"The human principle of self-respect, and the cultivation of human relationships, the behavior of Man towards Man, the attitude between people, that is really what theatre can offer. And from this very small unit, we can advance into the magnitude of world politics."

- Erwin Piscator

„Das menschliche Prinzip der Selbstachtung und die Pflege der menschlichen Beziehungen, the behavior of Man towards Man, das Verhalten von Mensch zu Mensch, das ist es, was eigentlich das Theater geben kann. Und von dieser kleinsten Einheit können wir auch in die weltpolitische Größe vorstoßen."

- Erwin Piscator

Erwin Piscator directs Richard Strauss' *Salome* at the Teatro Communale di Firenze in 19
Erwin Piscator während der Proben zu Richard Strauss' *Salome* am Teatro Communale in Florenz im Jahre 19

Erwin Piscator: The Legacy Continues
Erwin Piscator: Das Erbe lebt weiter

Text: Michael Lahr

In December 1985, Gregorij von Leïtis, Founder and Artistic Director of Elysium, instituted the Erwin Piscator Award to honor and commemorate the artistic and humanitarian legacy of the great theater man Erwin Piscator and his lasting influence on theater on both sides of the Atlantic. Like Leo Tolstoi, whose epic novel *War and Peace* Piscator adapted for the stage, he was convinced that "art only achieves its purpose, when it contributes to the improvement of man." Since the first award ceremony which took place on April 22, 1986 the Annual Erwin Piscator Award has been presented to artists, who – like Piscator – use the arts to contribute to the improvement of man. Ten years later in 1996, the Honorary Erwin Piscator Award in memory of Maria Ley Piscator was established to honor the extraordinary support of the arts and culture by individuals and institutions.

ERWIN PISCATOR: THE MAN AND THE ARTIST

Erwin Piscator, born on December 17, 1893, was a student of theater history with Artur Kutscher at Munich University, when the First World War started. He soon was called into the army, where he served as a signaler in a front-line infantry unit from the spring of 1915. The gruesome experiences of the Western Front shattered his whole outlook on the world. In his groundbreaking book *Das politische Theater (The Political Theater)*, first published in 1929 and later translated in many languages, he wrote: "My calendar begins on August 4, 1914. From that day the barometer rose: 13 million dead; 11 million crippled; 50 million soldiers who fought; 6 billion guns; 50 billion cubic meters of gas. How does 'personal growth' figure into that? Nobody is going to grow 'personally' there. Something else develops him. The twenty-year-old was confronted by War. Destiny. It made every other teacher superfluous."[1]

What Piscator lived through in the trenches in Flanders profoundly shaped his approach to theater.

In November 1918, right after the end of the First World War, Piscator came to Berlin. In the following years he became a great advocate of politics in the theater and a leading director of the Weimar Republic. On September 3, 1927, Piscator opened his first own theater company. Substantial backing for it came from the wealthy businessman

Ludwig Katzenellenbogen, to whom Piscator was introduced by the actress Tilla Durieux. But in June of 1928 the company was already bankrupt. However, within those ten months Piscator presented four productions, which became landmarks in theatrical history. The most famous one was *The Adventures of the Good Soldier Schwejk*. It established Piscator's international reputation.

Piscator wrote about his decision to transform Jaroslav Hašek's novel into a theater play: "The importance that the war has assumed in the literature of the last decade clearly reflects the great tensions within the social and intellectual development of Europe. Jaroslav Hašek's novel is remarkable in this context: other writers consciously 'make a stand' and attempt to formulate an attitude to the war, but the war in Hašek's novel cancels itself out. The war is seen through the temperament of the plain man. Schwejk is the triumph of common sense over the patriotic cliché. Hašek and his hero Schwejk stand outside the confines of tradition and accepted ideas, they defer to no conventions, so that what we see is the common man meeting mass murder and militarism, those joint affronts to nature, on a level at which sense becomes nonsense, heroism becomes ridiculous and the divine order of existence is turned into a grotesque madhouse."[2]

Piscator asked his friend George Grosz to create the set and draw a politico-satirical cartoon that could be projected onto a screen at the back of the stage.

In his diary of those days Piscator noted: "Grosz was sitting next to me. Suddenly he put his drawing pencil to paper. A cross was emerging. I can see it in front of me as if I was re-experiencing a dream: the incredibly assured stroke of his hand, his seismographic sensibility, the crystal-clear precision with which it directed the pencil across the paper: a body, a bent body, symbol of the tormented human body. Christ.
Suddenly Grosz pulls a soldier's boots up over the wounded feet, loosens the left hand, yanks it upwards, gives it a second cross. The first one had not been enough till now. So why not a second one?
And then: over the face, that two-thousand-year-old face of sorrows, he claps a gas mask.

Christ with a gas mask. A new Christ."[3]

Unfortunately, the rolls of film are lost. But some of George Grosz's still images survived.

As far as staging technique is concerned, the trick films, the cardboard marionettes and background projections and the sound editing were part of the special attraction the *Schwejk*-production held. But the reason why Piscator's production of *The Adventures of the Good Soldier Schwejk* made theater history is his ingenious use of two conveyor belts. On one of them Max Pallenberg as the soldier Schwejk would march endlessly through a world at war without, symbolically, getting anywhere. He would literally tread on one spot, while on the other conveyor belt the marionettes, milestones, outhouses and other things would glide by.

After *Schwejk* closed Piscator produced a number of other politically charged plays, such as *Konjunktur (Boom)*, a comedy of economics by Leo Lania, set in the international oil industry, Walther Mehring's inflation saga *Der Kaufmann von Berlin (The Merchant of Berlin)* with music by Hanns Eisler, and *§ 218*, Carl Credé's play dealing with the abortion paragraph of the German criminal code.

By the time, Piscator had premiered *§ 218*, a turning point had been reached: On October 3, 1929, the statesman Gustav Stresemann died. His death marked the end of six years of moderate politics in the Weimar Republic. Three weeks later Wall Street crashed and thus began a worldwide economic crisis. Inflation, unemployment and the weak democratic foundations of the Weimar Republic eventually brought Hitler to power.

In 1931 Piscator – invited by the Russian film company Meschrabpom – started work on his first and only film *The Revolt of the Fishermen*, which is based on a highly acclaimed novella by Anna Seghers. Seghers tells the story of the spontaneous uprising of fishermen against a monopoly. In the face of growing fascism, Piscator considered it absolutely necessary to create a strong united front against the threat of National Socialism. On October 5, 1934, when the film was finally shown for the first time, Hitler had already seized power. Piscator noted in his diary: "Hitler was faster – film lost its justification."

Piscator could not return to Germany. He went into exile to Paris in 1936, and on January 1, 1939 he and his second wife, Maria Ley, arrived in America.

There is a wonderful anecdote about Piscator's arrival in America, which he related in his diaries: "When our ship, the 'Franconia', arrived at this vast and strange continent, my heart felt scared and burdened. What should I do here? Start from scratch again? All over again? For the umpteenth time?
Behind my back: Hitler… And in front of me?
And now the immigration officer? He looks at my passport. Barely looks at me. Suddenly his greyblue eyes, his strong measured features lost all their formality and beamed with friendliness.
'A theater man,' he said, 'like … like Reinhardt?'
I nodded, and inwardly I thanked Max Reinhardt, who had prepared such a good reputation. 'Yes,' I said 'but not as famous…'
'Alas,' he sighed, 'You only have a permit for 8 months. If I could, I would give you one for two years, right away.'
'Thank you,' I stuttered… This man had for a moment pushed open the door to the freedom of democracy."[4]

The immigration quotas for actors, stage directors and such were low in the U.S. But for teachers they were much higher. Eventually Piscator accepted an offer by Dr. Alvin Johnson, founder and president of the New School for Social Research in New York and became Associate Professor of Dramatics. Dr. Johnson had organized one of the most extensive rescue operations in the social sciences and in the arts. Immediately after Hitler's seizure of power, Johnson founded a so-called university in exile which he incorporated into the New School for Social Research. Over the next few years, more than sixty scholars and artists from Germany, Austria, Hungary and Italy who were exiled by Hitler found refuge there.

At the New School, Piscator opened a Drama School, the so-called Dramatic Workshop. The faculty included the crème de la crème of the European theater world: writer Carl Zuckmayer, composer Hanns Eisler, and actor Fritz Kortner, among others. Piscator introduced an American audience to plays that had

never been seen in the U.S. before, including Lessing's *Nathan the Wise*.

Speaking of *Nathan the Wise*: this was Piscator's only production that went on to be shown at Broadway. The play premiered at the Studio Theater, an experimental stage in Greenwich Village, on March 11, 1942. Eventually it had a twenty-eight-day run at the Belasco Theatre, with Herbert Berghof playing the title part. Otherwise Piscator had a difficult time in the U.S. and with American theater.

Financial difficulties increased in the late 1940s and the political climate generated by Joseph McCarthy's anti-communist hysteria grew more and more hostile. When Piscator received a summons to appear before the House Un-American Activities Committee, he chose to leave America. On October 6, 1951 he went back to Europe and settled in West Germany. There, too, he faced many difficulties and was basically working as a guest director for an entire decade. Only in the spring of 1962, the Governing Mayor of Berlin, Willy Brandt, appointed Erwin Piscator as Intendant (Artistic Director) of the Freie Volksbühne (Free People's Theater) in West Berlin.

Piscator considered it to be the major task of contemporary German theater, to come to grips with the Hitler years. So he decided to direct the world-premiere of Rolf Hochhuth's *Der Stellvertreter (The Deputy)*. Hochhuth's play – which opened on February 2, 1963 – takes the Catholic Church and Pope Pius XII to task over its silence during the Holocaust.

With Hochhuth and later on with Peter Weiss' *Die Ermittlung (The Investigation* dealing with the Frankfurt Auschwitz trials), with Heinar Kipphardt's play *In der Sache J. Robert Oppenheimer (In the Matter of J. Robert Oppenheimer*, dealing with the development of the American atomic bomb and the responsibility of the scientist toward society and history), and with Hans Hellmut Kirst's *Der Aufstand der Offiziere (The Uprising of the Officers*, a dramatic treatment of the aborted attempt to assassinate Adolf Hitler on July 20, 1944), Piscator had found the congenial playwrights that helped him create a new form of a politically relevant theater: the documentary theater. During the rehearsals for Kirst's *The Uprising of the Officers*, Piscator was taken to the hospital. He died shortly after the play's premiere on March 30, 1966.

PISCATOR'S INNOVATIONS

What is it that made Piscator such a great and original theater man? – What is immediately obvious is Piscator's creative use of all the new technologies that were available to him: Sound, trick film, documentary footage, complicated stage constructions, using elements that could be shifted and turned, thus enabling him to play out various scenes simultaneously on stage. Piscator also made extensive and innovative use of lighting equipment. I am sure, he would have been thrilled to see what today in our digital computer-era is possible in terms of stage effects. Today, Piscator's technological inventions are being used in theaters all over the world.

But there is more. The imprint of Piscator's way of theater can mostly be observed in the Off-Broadway and Off-Off-Broadway theater. Known for their social and political engagement and their interest in improvisation and experimentation, those theatrical movements owe very much to Piscator. One such Off-Off-Broadway group are we, Elysium. Since its foundation in 1983 by Gregorij von Leïtis, Elysium has staged numerous American premieres of new German plays. But more than that: Sharing Piscator's belief, that theater is a means for social and political change, Gregorij von Leïtis founded the program *Theater for Homeless* and to this day strives to integrate minorities by means of theater.

Other people should be named here, too. An extraordinary group of theater artists studied, in Piscator's Dramatic Workshop at the New School: Marlon Brando, Tennessee Williams, Tony Curtis, Judith Malina, Rod Steiger, Harry Belafonte, Anthony Franciosa, Ben Gazzara, Walter Matthau, Tony Randall, Shelley Winters, Elaine Stritch, to just name a few. Some of them later on founded theater companies of their own, among them Judith Malina, and Tony Randall.

But there is still more. Piscator's most important invention was what he called Epic

Leo Kerz' stage design for Piscator's production of Rolf Hochhuth's *The Deputy*
Bühnenbildentwurf von Leo Kerz für Piscators Inszenierung von Rolf Hochhuths *Der Stellvertreter*

Theater. On the surface, the term Epic Theater means, that an epic novel is dramatized and turned into a sequence of scenes. At the same time, Epic Theater denounces the "well-made play" and rather presents a sequence of episodes. Thus the spectator cannot be put under the spell of a magic illusion, something Max Reinhardt was perfect at. Piscator called himself a disenchanter. He never grew tired to scream his Cassandra cry in the face of what was happening around him. The Epic Theater does not appeal to the emotions of the spectator. Instead it wants to keep his critical mind awake and challenge him to think, thus turning the theatre into a forum for political argumentation.

Now the reader will probably say: This sounds exactly like Bertolt Brecht's theory. – That's right. Brecht, who worked with Piscator on the dramatization of *Schwejk* and other plays, created the theoretical foundation, but Piscator was the first to actually make Epic Theater. Brecht admitted that Piscator had been his teacher. And Brecht in his writings, which were published shortly after Piscator's death, says about Piscator: "He is the greatest theater man of all time. He will leave a legacy which we should use."

RELEVANCE OF POLITICAL THEATRE TODAY

Another term for "Epic Theater" is "Political Theater". So in closing let me briefly ask: What, if any, is the relevance of Political Theater today?

Piscator somewhere says: "For lack of phantasy most people do not fully experience their own lives, let alone the world. Otherwise reading just one page of the newspaper would be sufficient for mankind to start a rebellion. Stronger means are thus necessary. One of them is the theater."[5]

Political theater in this sense is a theater that serves as a wake-up call, a theater that questions our way of thinking, talking, and judging. A theater that exposes the manipulation going on around us – in the media, in politics, everywhere; a theater that reveals the structural flaws of our man-made institutions and corporations. The topics of political theater today are manifold: They range from unemployment and poverty, to racism, religious bigotry, exploitation of our natural resources at a deadly speed etc. In the end it all burns down to one single pursuit: The respect of each of us for our fellow human-beings. Piscator summarized it beautifully when he symbolically received the keys to the Freie Volksbühne in Berlin in 1962: "Let us glorify man! Let us instill him with the most holy of all sentiments: The reverence of man for man! This is our quest. This shall be our goal!"[6]

1. Erwin Piscator: Das Politische Theater, Reinbek 1963, p. 25
2. Ibidem, p. 179
3. Lothar Fischer: George Grosz mit Selbstzeugnissen und Bilddokumenten, Reinbek 1989, p. 97f.
4. Erwin Piscator: Amerika, printed in: Knut Boeser, Renata Vatková (Ed.): Erwin Piscator. Eine Arbeitsbiographie in 2 Bänden, Berlin 1986, vol. 2, p. 44
5. Das Programm der Piscatorbühne. No 1, September 1927. Hoppla, wir leben! von Ernst Toller. Edited by Piscatorbühne. Berlin 1927, p. 5.
6. Erwin Piscator: Schriften II. Aufsätze Reden Gespräche, Berlin 1968, p. 310

Im Dezember 1985 rief Gregorij von Leïtis, Gründer und Intendant von Elysium, den Erwin Piscator Preis ins Leben, um das künstlerische und menschliche Erbe des großen Theatermannes Erwin Piscator und seinen bleibenden Einfluß auf das Theater auf beiden Seiten des Atlantiks zu ehren und die Erinnerung an ihn wachzuhalten. Wie Leo Tolstoi, dessen epischen Roman *Krieg und Frieden* er für die Bühne bearbeitet hatte, war Piscator überzeugt: „Die Kunst hat nur dann Zweck, wenn sie zur Verbesserung des Menschen beiträgt." Seit der ersten Preisverleihung am 22. April 1986 wird der jährliche Erwin Piscator Preis an Künstler vergeben, die – wie Piscator – die Künste gebrauchen, um ihren Beitrag zur Verbesserung des Menschen zu leisten. Zehn Jahre später, 1996, wurde der Erwin Piscator Ehrenpreis in Erinnerung an Maria Ley Piscator aus der Taufe gehoben, um damit Persönlichkeiten und Institutionen zu würdigen, die in besonderer Weise Kunst und Kultur unterstützen.

Erwin Piscator

ERWIN PISCATOR: DER MENSCH UND DER KÜNSTLER

Erwin Piscator, geboren am 17. Dezember 1893, war Student der Theaterwissenschaften bei Artur Kutscher an der Münchner Universität, als der 1. Weltkrieg ausbrach. Schon bald wurde er in die Armee eingezogen und diente vom Frühjahr 1915 an als Funker einer Infanterie-Einheit an der Front. Die grauenhaften Erlebnisse an der Westfront erschütterten sein Lebensbild grundlegend. In seinem bahnbrechenden Buch *Das politische Theater*, erstmals erschienen 1929 und später in viele Sprachen übersetzt, schreibt er: „Meine Zeitrechnung beginnt am 4. August 1914. Von da ab stieg das Barometer: 13 Millionen Tote, 11 Millionen Krüppel, 50 Millionen Soldaten, die marschierten, 6 Milliarden Geschosse, 50 Milliarden Kubikmeter Gas. Was ist da ‚persönliche Entwicklung'? Niemand entwickelt sich da ‚persönlich'. Da entwickelt etwas anderes ihn. Vor dem Zwanzigjährigen erhob sich der Krieg. Schicksal. Es machte jeden anderen Lehrmeister überflüssig."[1]

Was Piscator in den Schützengräben in Flandern durchmachte, prägte seine Einstellung zum Theater maßgeblich.

Im November 1918, direkt nach dem Ende des 1. Weltkrieges, kommt Piscator nach Berlin. In den folgenden Jahren wird er ein Verfechter der Politik im Theater und einer der führenden Regisseure der Weimarer Republik. Am 3. September 1927 öffnete Piscator seine erste eigene Bühne. Erhebliche Unterstützung erhielt er von dem wohlhabenden Geschäftsmann Ludwig Katzenellenbogen, den er durch die Schauspielerin Tilla Durieux kennengelernt hatte. Schon im Juni 1928 war sein Ensemble bankrott. Doch innerhalb dieser zehn Monate inszenierte Piscator vier Stücke, die zu Meilensteinen der Theatergeschichte wurden. Die bekannteste dieser Inszenierungen war *Die Abenteuer des braven Soldaten Schwejk*. Sie etablierte Piscators internationalen Ruhm.

Über seine Entscheidung, Jaroslav Hašeks Roman zu einem Bühnenstück zu machen, schrieb Piscator: „Die Bedeutung, die der Krieg in der Dichtung des letzten Jahrzehnts erworben hat, spiegelt deutlich die großen Spannungen in der sozialen und geistigen Entwicklung Europas. Während aber andere Dichter zum Krieg ‚Stellung nehmen', sich mit ihm auseinandersetzen, ist der Roman Jaroslav Hašeks bemerkenswert, weil in ihm der Krieg, man könnte sagen, sich selbst aufhebt. Hier ist der Krieg gesehen durch das Temperament des schlichten Mannes. Der Schwejk ist ein Triumph des gesunden Menschenverstandes über die Phrase. Da Hašek und sein Held Schwejk jenseits aller überkommenen und anerkannten Begriffe, jenseits jeder Konvention stehen, so erleben wir hier die Konfrontation des einfachen Menschen mit der Unnatur des Massenmordes und des Militarismus auf jener Ebene, wo sich jeder Sinn in Unsinn, aller Heroismus in Lächerlichkeit und die göttliche Weltordnung in ein groteskes Irrenhaus verwandelt."[2]

Piscator bat seinen Freund George Grosz, das Bühnenbild zu schaffen und einen politisch-satirischen Comic zu zeichnen, der auf die Rückwand der Bühne projiziert werden konnte.

In seinem Tagebuch notiert Piscator: „Grosz saß neben mir. Plötzlich setzte er seinen Zeichenstift an. Es entstand ein Kreuz. Ich sehe es vor mir, wie im Nacherlebnis eines

Maria Ley Piscator (right) and Michael Lahr in September of 1992
Maria Ley Piscator (rechts) und Michael Lahr im September 1992

Traums: den unglaublich sicheren Duktus seiner Hand, die kristallklare Präzision, mit der sie den Stift über das Papier führte: einen Leib, einen gekrümmten Leib, Symbol des geschundenen Menschenkörpers. Christus. Plötzlich zieht Grosz ihm über die wunden Füße Soldatenstiefel, löst die linke Hand, reißt sie nach oben, gibt ihr ein zweites Kreuz. Das eine hatte bisher nicht ausgereicht. Warum also nicht ein zweites. Und dann: Über das Gesicht, über das zweitausend Jahre alte Leidensgesicht stülpt er eine Gasmaske. Christus mit der Gasmaske. Ein neuer Christus."[3]

Leider sind die Filmrollen verloren. Doch einige Bilder von Grosz sind erhalten.

Was die Bühnentechnik betrifft, waren der Zeichentrickfilm, die Pappfiguren und Hintergrundprojektionen und die Klangeffekte zweifellos Teil der besonderen Attraktion der Schwejk-Produktion. Der Grund aber, warum Piscators Inszenierung von *Die Abenteuer des braven Soldaten Schwejk* Theatergeschichte schrieb ist seine geniale Verwendung zweier Laufbänder: Auf dem einen marschiert Max Pallenberg als Soldat Schwejk endlos durch eine Welt im Krieg, ohne – symbolisch – je irgendwo anzukommen. Er tritt im wörtlichen Sinn auf der Stelle, während auf einem anderen Laufband Puppen, Kilometersteine, Plumpsklos und andere Dinge an ihm vorbeiziehen.

Nach der Schwejk-Produktion brachte Piscator eine Reihe von politisch aufgeladenen Stücken auf die Bühne, darunter die in der internationalen Ölindustrie spielende Wirtschaftssatire *Konjunktur* von Leo Lania, Walther Mehrings Inflationsgeschichte *Der Kaufmann von Berlin* mit Musik von Hanns Eisler, und *§ 218*, Carl Credes Stück über den Abtreibungsparagraphen des deutschen Strafgesetzbuches.

Als *§ 218* seine Premiere hatte, war ein Wendepunkt erreicht: Am 3. Oktober 1929 starb der Politiker und Friedensnobelpreisträger Gustav Stresemann. Sein Tod markierte das Ende einer sechsjährigen Phase moderater Politik in der Weimarer Republik. Drei Wochen später kam es zum Crash an der Wall Street. Die Weltwirtschaftskrise begann. Inflation, Arbeitslosigkeit und schwache demokratische Strukturen der Weimarer Republik brachten schließlich Hitler an die Macht.

1931 begann Piscator – auf Einladung der russischen Filmgesellschaft Meschrabpom – mit der Arbeit an seinem ersten und einzigen Film *Der Aufstand der Fischer*, basierend auf der bekannten Novelle von Anna Seghers. Das Buch erzählt die Geschichte einer spontanen Erhebung von Fischern gegen ein Monopol. Angesichts des zunehmenden Faschismus hielt Piscator es für unbedingt notwendig, eine starke vereinte Front gegen die Bedrohung des Nationalsozialismus zu schaffen. Am 5. Oktober 1934, als sein Film endlich erstaufgeführt wurde, war Hitler schon an der Macht. Piscator schrieb in sein Tagebuch: „Hitler war schneller – Film hat seine Berechtigung verloren."

Piscator konnte nicht nach Deutschland zurückkehren. Stattdessen ging er 1936 nach Paris ins Exil. Am 1. Januar 1939 landete er mit seiner zweiten Frau Maria Ley in Amerika.

Eine wunderbare Anekdote über seine Ankunft in Amerika hat Piscator seinem Tagebuch anvertraut: „Als sich das Schiff – die ‚Franconia' – dem großen, fremden Kontinent näherte, wurde mir schwer und angst zumute.

Was sollte ich dort? Noch einmal anfangen? Wieder noch einmal ganz von vorne – zum wievielten Male war das? […] Hinter einem Hitler… vor einem – ?

Und nun der Beamte? Er blättert in meinem Paß. Kaum schaut er auf. Und sein blaugraues Auge, sein regelmäßiges, stark amerikanisches Gesicht hatte jede Formalität, die wie ich zuvor schon festgestellt hatte, keineswegs der einer deutschen Physiognomie glich, verloren – und strahlte von Freundlichkeit.

‚Theatermann', sagte er, ‚ so – so ein Reinhardt?'

Ich nickte und war Reinhardt im Stillen dankbar, der mir eine so gute Reputation gemacht hatte. ‚Ja, aber nicht so berühmt…' sagte ich.

‚Ach', seufzte er, ‚Sie haben ja nur eine 8-Monate-Aufenthaltsgenehmigung. Wenn ich könnte, gleich hier, möchte ich Ihnen zwei Jahre geben.'

‚Danke', stotterte ich, ganz benommen von dieser Überraschung, und plötzlich schien die Sonne von innen her die Fenster der Wolkenkratzer zu erleuchten… Dieser Mann hatte das Tor zur Freiheit der Demokratie, so schien es mir, in diesem Augenblick aufgestoßen."[4]

Das Einwanderungskontingent für Schauspieler, Regisseure und andere Bühnenkünstler war klein. Aber für Lehrer war es sehr viel größer. Schließlich akzeptierte Piscator ein Angebot von Dr. Alvin Johnson, dem Gründer und Präsidenten der New School for Social Research in New York, und wurde Dozent der Theaterwissenschaft. Dr. Johnson hatte eine der größten und umfangreichsten Rettungsmaßnahmen für die Sozialwissenschaften und Künste organisiert. Direkt nach Hitlers Machtergreifung hatte er die sogenannte Universität im Exil ins Leben gerufen, die er der New School angliederte. Über die nächsten Jahre fanden mehr als 60 Wissenschaftler und Künstler aus Deutschland, Österreich, Ungarn und Italien dort eine neue Wirkungsstätte.

An der New School öffnete Piscator eine Schauspielschule, den Dramatic Workshop. Zum Lehrkörper gehörte die crème de la crème der europäischen Theaterwelt: der Schriftsteller Carl Zuckmayer, der Komponist Hanns Eisler, der Schauspieler Fritz Kortner und viele andere. Piscator stellte dem amerikanischen Publikum Stücke vor, die bis dahin in den USA nicht aufgeführt worden waren, darunter auch *Nathan der Weise.*

À propos *Nathan der Weise*: Dies war Piscators einzige Produktion, die an den Broadway gelangte. Am 11. März 1942 eröffnete das Stück im Studio Theater, einer experimentellen Bühne in Greenwich Village. Schließlich hatte es einen 28tägigen Run im Belasco Theater, mit Herbert Berghof in der Titelrolle. Ansonsten hatte Piscator in den USA und mit dem amerikanischen Theater eher seine Schwierigkeiten.

Die finanziellen Probleme nahmen in den späten 1940er Jahren zu, und das durch Joseph McCarthys antikommunistische Hysterie geprägte politische Klima wurde immer feindseliger. Als Piscator die Aufforderung erhielt, vor dem Ausschuß für unamerikanische Umtriebe des Repräsentantenhauses zu erscheinen, entschloß er sich, Amerika zu verlassen. Am 6. Oktober 1951 kehrte er nach Europa zurück und ließ sich in Westdeutschland nieder. Doch auch dort hatte er es nicht leicht und war quasi zehn Jahre lang als Gastregisseur tätig. Erst im Frühjahr 1962 übertrug Berlins Regierender Bürgermeister Willy Brandt Erwin Piscator die Intendanz der Freien Volksbühne in West-Berlin.

Für Piscator bestand die wichtigste Aufgabe des zeitgenössischen deutschen Theaters darin, sich mit der Hitler-Zeit auseinander zu setzen. Deshalb entschied er sich, die Welturaufführung von Rolf Hochhuths *Der Stellvertreter* zu inszenieren. Hochhuths Stück, das am 20. Februar 1963 Premiere hatte, befasst sich mit dem Schweigen Papst Pius XII. und der katholischen Kirche während des Holocaust.

Mit Hochhuth, und später mit Peter Weiss (dessen Stück *Die Ermittlung* sich mit den

Frankfurter Ausschwitzprozessen beschäftigte), Heinar Kipphardt (der in seinem Stück *In der Sache J. Robert Oppenheimer* die Entwicklung der amerikanischen Atombombe und die Verantwortung des Wissenschaftlers gegenüber der Gesellschaft und der Geschichte thematisierte) und mit Hans Hellmut Kirst (der in seinem Stück *Der Aufstand der Offiziere* den gescheiterten Attentatsversuch auf Hitler vom 20. Juli 1944 beleuchtete), hatte Piscator wesensverwandte Dramatiker gefunden, die ihm halfen, eine neue Form des politisch relevanten Theaters zu schaffen: Das Dokumentartheater. Während der Proben zu Kirsts *Der Aufstand der Offiziere* wurde Piscator ins Krankenhaus gebracht. Er starb kurz nach der Premiere am 30. März 1966.

PISCATORS NEUERUNGEN

Worin liegt die Größe und Originalität des Theatermanns Piscator? – Was auf den ersten Blick ersichtlich ist, ist Piscators kreativer Einsatz all der neuen Technologien, die ihm zur Verfügung standen: Ton, Trickfilm, Dokumentarfilmaufnahmen, komplizierte Bühnenkonstrukte, der Einsatz von Elementen, die sich drehten und bewegten, so dass er verschiedene Szenen gleichzeitig auf der Bühne spielen lassen konnte. Auch von der neuesten Lichttechnik machte Piscator reichlich Gebrauch. Er wäre sicher begeistert gewesen von den Bühneneffekten, die im digitalen Computer-Zeitalter möglich sind. Heute werden Piscators bühnentechnische Erfindungen in Theatern rund um die Welt genutzt.

Doch das ist nicht alles. Piscators Art des Theaters hat im Off-Broadway und Off-Off-Broadway tiefe Spuren hinterlassen. Diese beiden Theaterbewegungen, die charakterisiert sind durch soziales und politisches Engagement und ihren Hang zur Improvisation und zum Experimentellen, verdanken Piscator sehr viel. Eine solche Off-Off-Broadway Gruppe sind wir, Elysium. Seit seiner Gründung 1983 durch Gregorij von Leïtis hat Elysium etliche amerikanische Erstaufführungen deutscher Stücke auf die Bühne gebracht. Doch mehr noch: Wie Piscator ist Gregorij von Leïtis davon überzeugt, dass Theater ein gutes Mittel für sozialen und politischen Wandel ist; und deshalb gründete er das Theater für Obdachlose und bemüht sich bis heute, Minderheiten durch theatralisch-künstlerische Arbeit zu integrieren.

Auch andere Menschen sollten hier genannt

Bill-board of the world premiere of Peter Weiss' play *The Investigation*
Plakat der Uraufführung von Peter Weiss' Stück *Die Ermittlung*

Bill-board of Piscator's last production
Plakat von Piscators letzter Inszenierung

werden. Eine ungewöhnliche Gruppe von Bühnenkünstlern studierte in Piscators Dramatic Workshop: Marlon Brando, Tennessee Williams, Tony Curtis, Judith Malina, Rod Steiger, Harry Belafonte, Anthony Franciosa, Ben Gazzara, Walter Matthau, Tony Randall, Shelley Winters, Elaine Stritch, um nur einige zu nennen. Einige gründeten später eigene Theatergruppen, etwa Judith Malina und Tony Randall.

Doch auch damit nicht genug. Piscators wichtigste Neuerung war das, was er „episches Theater" nannte. Oberflächlich betrachtet bedeutet episches Theater, dass ein epischer Roman dramatisiert und in eine Folge von Szenen übertragen wird. Gleichzeitig bricht das epische Theater mit dem perfekt durchorganisierten Stück und präsentiert eher eine Aneinanderreihung von Episoden. Dadurch kann der Zuschauer nicht dem Bann einer magischen Illusion erliegen, eine Ausdrucksform, die Max Reinhardt perfektioniert hatte. Piscator nannte sich selbst einen Entzauberer. Er wurde nie müde, seinen Kassandra-Ruf hinauszuschreien. Das epische Theater wendet sich nicht an die Gefühle der Zuschauer. Es will vielmehr ihren kritischen Geist wecken und fordert sie zum Denken auf. Dadurch wird das Theater zum Forum der politischen Debatte.

Jetzt wird der Leser vermutlich entgegnen: Das klingt genau wie Bertolt Brechts Theorie. – Das ist richtig. Brecht, der mit Piscator an der Dramatisierung des *Schwejk* und anderer Stücke arbeitete, schuf das theoretische Fundament, doch Piscator war der erste, der tatsächlich episches Theater machte. Brecht räumte später ein, dass Piscator sein Lehrer war. Und in seinen Schriften, die kurz nach Piscators Tod veröffentlicht wurden, sagt Brecht über Piscator: „Er ist der größte Theatermann aller Zeiten. Er wird ein Erbe hinterlassen, das wir nutzen sollten."

Piscator sagt irgendwo: „Aus Mangel an Phantasie erleben die meisten Menschen nicht einmal ihr eigenes Leben, geschweige denn ihre Welt. Sonst müßte die Lektüre eines einzigen Zeitungsblattes genügen, um die Menschheit in Aufruhr zu bringen. Es sind also stärkere Mittel nötig. Eins davon ist das Theater."[5]

Politisches Theater in diesem Sinne dient als Weckruf, es ist ein Theater, das unsere Denkgewohnheiten, unser Reden und Urteil in Frage stellt. Ein Theater, das die Manipulation anprangert, die um uns herum geschieht – in den Medien, in der Politik, überall; ein Theater, das die strukturellen Schwächen unserer von Menschen gemachten Institutionen und Firmen offenlegt. Die Themen eines solchen politischen Theaters heute sind vielfältig: Sie reichen von Arbeitslosigkeit und Armut, über Rassismus, Bigotterie, Ausbeutung unserer natürlichen Ressourcen in tödlicher Geschwindigkeit usw. Am Ende geht es um die Verfolgung eines einzigen Zieles: Der Respekt eines jeden von uns vor seinen Mitmenschen. Piscator fasste dies wunderbar zusammen, als er 1962 symbolisch die Schlüssel der Freien Volksbühne in Berlin erhielt: „Verherrlichen wir den Menschen! Flößen wir ihm das heiligste aller Gefühle ein: Ehrfurcht des Menschen vor dem Menschen! Dem gilt unser Streben. Das sei unser Ziel!"[6]

1. Erwin Piscator: Das Politische Theater, Reinbek 1963, S. 25
2. Ebd., S. 179
3. Lothar Fischer: George Grosz mit Selbstzeugnissen und Bilddokumenten, Reinbek 1989, S. 97f.
4. Erwin Piscator: Amerika, abgedruckt in: Knut Boeser, Renata Vatková (Hg.): Erwin Piscator. Eine Arbeitsbiographie in 2 Bänden, Berlin 1986, Bd. 2, S. 44
5. Das Programm der Piscatorbühne. Nummer 1, September 1927. Hoppla, wir leben! von Ernst Toller. Hrsg. von der Piscatorbühne. Berlin 1927, S. 5.
6. Erwin Piscator: Schriften II. Aufsätze Reden Gespräche, Berlin 1968, S. 310

DIE BEDEUTUNG DES POLITISCHEN THEATERS HEUTE

Politisches Theater ist ein anderer Begriff für Episches Theater. Zum Schluß will ich kurz fragen: Was – wenn überhaupt – ist die Bedeutung des politischen Theaters heute?

Maria Ley Piscator (1898 - 1999) in front of the Piscator House on New York's Upper East Side
Maria Ley Piscator (1898 - 1999) vor dem Piscator Haus in der 76. Straße auf New Yorks Upper East Side

The Beginning of a Never-Ending Friendship
Der Beginn einer endlosen Freundschaft

Text: Gregorij H. von Leïtis   Translation: Christine Schurtman

It was the beginning of December 1985 in New York. I had returned a few days earlier from the funeral of my beloved Mam in Munich. New York in the snow: A white blanket covered the city as if it wanted to hide all hurt, all pain, and all misery for a moment. One moment to allow forgetting – and to make room for something new. It made me feel good to experience this city as so peaceful, so fragile and sensitive.

With these thoughts and images I arrived at the Goethe House, where Dr. Christoph Wecker, the director of the Institute, had invited people for a celebration in honor of Erwin Piscator, who had died on March 30, 1966. Piscator's only film *The Revolt of the Fishermen*, was also to be shown. Fewer people than I had expected were present. The young people were missing. Among the former exiles, the "German-speaking colony" in New York, I discovered Dolly Haas, Henry Marx, editor of the German-Jewish newspaper *Aufbau*, Mimi Grossberg, Christiane Zimmer (Hugo von Hofmannsthal's daughter), and the daughter of Mies van der Rohe. Hans Sahl, the loyal old friend, was also there. I found him in conversation with a graceful, vivacious, still very young-acting lady – Maria Ley Piscator. I heard a friendly voice intruding into my

thoughts: "Good evening. Finally I see you again, who has neglected until now to call me!" At that moment it became apparent to me, that a friendship would begin that evening, which was to teach me a lot and show me new paths.

So that's who she was: Maria Ley Piscator, the widow of the theatre director Erwin Piscator, a legend to the German-speaking colony of New York. Here she was, facing me with her radiant eyes, the charming smile, a shawl elegantly draped over her shoulders, held together by a large brooch. The hand she extended to me seemed like precious porcelain to me, and yet great energy and strength emanated from it.

With many sentences I asked her pardon and ended with: "Why should I have called you? There was no reason...", which she countered laughingly with: "From now on there is a reason! We will work together."

That seemed rather far-fetched, and I filed it under: benevolent old lady, wants to say something nice to me, so I'll feel comfortable around her. She said it with much warmth and without any arrogance, so that I would have loved to accept.

14

But life in New York had taught me that things easily come out of people's mouths which later are translated into deeds only with difficulty or not at all. So I didn't put much faith into her words, especially since I knew that Maria Ley Piscator was surrounded by many sycophants, all people who wanted something from her, whom she gathered around herself like courtiers. She moved those people back and forth as if they were on rubber bands. Sometimes the band snapped and the fall could be painful. I didn't want to belong to those courtiers – people I called "ermine moths" to myself.

The evening was stimulating. Maria was full of charm, wit, and a deeper seriousness – in the manner of children who have the freedom of carefree movement, and yet sense that there is still a time of maturity in their future, which they co-determine. With Maria Piscator the result was a refreshing youthfulness – in spite of her 87 years.

We made a date for lunch for the following day in her apartment. I did not yet know at that point, that an important stage in my life was about to begin. I arrived punctually at 12 noon at the Piscator house on 76ᵗʰ Street. Don – Maria Piscator's secretary – opened the door – in this devout posture I always find so weird with this exaggerated friendliness, which after all is only expression of a mood; and one knows that one is powerless when confronted with his moods: A figure Genet describes so appropriately in his *Maids*. It's the kind of person who trusts himself only with a second-hand life, and who simply accepts everything with resignation for fear of taking a fall which could deprive him of his life.

There I stood in the reception room-study and was announced. A perfect stage setting, I thought. The head of a Greek youth stood on a pillar pasted over with marbled paper – one of the antique heads of a youth so often copied in the 18ᵗʰ and 19ᵗʰ century. On the walls were framed stage designs by Gropius, photos of Erwin Piscator; in between stood heavy mirrors of medium height arranged like partitions; and in the middle was a long table piled high with books, surrounded by Biedermeier chairs from Vienna. A life – her life – compactly packed into one room. Through a narrow corridor I was led into the salon, or library,

to "Madame," to Maria Ley Piscator. As she came towards me and extended her hand in greeting, she seemed to me like a long-forgotten Europe – I felt a magic, which I didn't want to explain to myself – a beautiful beginning.

She personified the old Europe, which encompassed so much: forms of conversation, mutual respect and courtesy, an attempt at inclusivity as it was then customary in cosmopolitan and educated social circles of the time, an internationality, which one doesn't encounter any more today in spite of all our mobility.

In the time between the wars and after the Second World War it was evidently possible to destroy such cultivated specimens completely. They've become characters in novels. But here I was confronted with such a rare, precious specimen – what a gift! In barely an hour she led me through her history – for me an infinite story, which doesn't end, and never will end, and will always find other forms of surviving. In the course of this encounter, Maria Piscator made it clear to me that she was serious about cooperation, and I agreed. A journey began, with many colors and new impressions, such as only a child or an eternally curious person can offer.

Maria Ley Piscator (right) and Gregorij von Leïtis
Maria Ley Piscator (rechts) und Gregorij von Leïtis

Maria Ley Piscator once called herself a "mirror child," who reflects, a reflection of eternal enchantment, of eternal mystery. It was a present for me to discover something of this mystery, to see the reality which is the mirror child Maria, who was able to light the true way and who also led one astray so playfully.

Maria Piscator is a constant challenge in the search for truth – for the third dimension.

Es war Anfang Dezember 1985 in New York, ich war wenige Tage zuvor von der Beerdigung meiner geliebten Mam aus München zurückgekehrt.

Das verschneite New York. Eine weiße Decke legte sich über die Stadt, als wollte sie alle Verletzungen, allen Schmerz und alles Elend für einen Moment zudecken. Einen Moment, um vergessen zu lassen – Platz zu schaffen für etwas Neues. Es tat mir gut, diese Stadt so friedlich, so zerbrechlich und empfindsam zu erleben.

Mit diesen Gedanken und Bildern kam ich im Goethe House an, wohin Dr. Christoph Wecker, der Leiter des Instituts, zu einer Feierstunde zu Ehren des 1966 verstorbenen Erwin Piscator eingeladen hatte. Es sollte auch Piscators einziger Film *Der Aufstand der Fischer* gezeigt werden.

Es waren weniger Leute da, als ich erwartet hatte, es fehlten die jungen Menschen. Unter den ehemaligen Exilanten der „deutschsprachigen Kolonie" in New York entdeckte ich Dolly Haas, Henry Marx, Chefredakteur vom *Aufbau*, Mimi Grossberg, Christiane Zimmer (die Tochter Hugo von Hofmannsthals) und die Tochter von Mies van der Rohe.

Auch der treue alte Freund Hans Sahl war da. Ich fand ihn im Gespräch mit der zierlichen, noch sehr jugendlich wirkenden Maria Ley Piscator. In meine Gedanken hinein hörte ich eine freundliche Stimme sagen: „Guten Abend! Nun sehe ich Sie auch einmal wieder, der es bis heute versäumt hat, mich anzurufen." In dem Moment wurde mir klar, dass an diesem Abend eine Freundschaft beginnen würde, die mich vieles lehren und mir neue Wege aufzeigen sollte.

Das also war sie: Maria Ley Piscator, die

Witwe des Theaterregisseurs Erwin Piscator, eine Legende in der deutschsprachigen Kolonie von New York. Da stand sie vor mir, mit ihren strahlenden Augen, dem charmanten Lächeln, einen Schal elegant über die Schulter geworfen, der von einer großen Brosche zusammengehalten wurde.

Die Hand, die sie mir reichte, erschien mir wie kostbares Porzellan, und dennoch ging von ihr große Energie und Kraft aus.

Ich entschuldigte mich mit vielen Sätzen und endete mit einem: „Warum hätte ich Sie anrufen sollen? Es gab keinen Grund…", worauf sie lachend konterte: „Von nun an gibt es einen Grund! Wir werden zusammen arbeiten."

Das erschien mir doch recht überzogen, ich ordnete es ein unter: Wohlwollende alte Dame, möchte mir etwas Nettes sagen, damit ich mich in ihrer Umgebung wohlfühle. Sie sagte das mit viel Wärme und ganz ohne Anmaßung, so dass ich es gerne angenommen hätte.

Doch das Leben in New York hatte mich gelehrt, dass Lippen leicht etwas loslassen, was später schwer oder gar nicht in die Tat umgesetzt wird.

Also maß ich ihren Worten keine Bedeutung bei, zumal ich wusste, dass Maria Ley Piscator von vielen Schmeichlern umgeben war, Leuten, die alle etwas von ihr wollten und die sie wie einen Hofstaat um sich sammelte.

Sie bewegte diese Leute hin und her wie an einem Gummiband. Manchmal riß auch so ein Band, und der Sturz konnte schmerzhaft sein.

Der Abend verlief anregend. Maria war voller Charme, Witz und tieferem Ernst – nach Art der Kinder, die die Freiheit haben, sich sorglos zu bewegen und dabei doch ahnen, dass eine Zeit der Reife noch vor ihnen liegt, die sie mitbestimmen können. Bei Maria Piscator war das Ergebnis eine erfrischende Jugendlichkeit – trotz ihrer 87 Jahre.

Wir verabredeten uns für den nächsten Tag zum Lunch in ihrer Wohnung. Ich wusste zu diesem Zeitpunkt noch nicht, dass damit eine wichtige Stufe in meinem Leben beginnen sollte.

Pünktlich um 12 Uhr kam ich im Piscator-House in der 76. Straße an. Don, Maria Piscators Sekretär, öffnete die Tür – in dieser mir stets unheimlichen devoten Haltung, mit dieser übertriebenen Freundlichkeit, die doch

Maria Ley Piscator in her New York apartment in the 1980s
Maria Ley Piscator in den 1980er Jahren in ihrer New Yorker Wohnung

nur Ausdruck einer Laune ist, wobei man weiß, dass man machtlos gegenüber seinen Launen ist – eine Figur, wie sie Genet so trefflich in seinen *Zofen* beschreibt. Es ist die Sorte Mensch, die sich nur ein Leben aus zweiter Hand zutrauen und aus Angst vor dem Sturz, der ihnen ihr Leben rauben könnte, einfach alles als gegeben hinnehmen.

Da stand ich nun im Empfangs- und Arbeitszimmer und wurde gemeldet. Ein perfektes Theaterset, ging es mir durch den Kopf.

Auf einer mit marmoriertem Papier verklebten Säule stand der Kopf eines griechischen Jünglings – einer der im 18. und 19. Jahrhundert viel kopierten Jünglingsköpfe aus der Antike, an den Wänden gerahmte Bühnenbildentwürfe von Gropius, Fotos von Erwin Piscator, dazwischen schwere halbhohe Spiegel, aufgestellt wie Trennwände – und in der Mitte ein mit Büchern vollgeladener langer Tisch, umgeben von Biedermeierstühlen aus Wien. Ein Leben – ihr Leben – kurz und bündig in einen Raum gepackt.

Über einen schmalen Gang wurde ich in den Salon, oder auch Bibliothek, geführt – zu „Madame", zu Maria Ley Piscator.

Wie sie da auf mich zukam und mir die Hand zum Gruß reichte, erschien sie mir wie ein lang vergessenes Europa – ich empfand einen Zauber, den ich mir gar nicht erklären konnte – ein wunderbarer Beginn.

Sie verkörperte das alte Europa, das so vieles umfasste: Formen der Konversation, der Achtung und Höflichkeit voreinander, den Versuch der Nichtausgrenzung, wie es üblich war in den damaligen kosmopolitischen und gebildeten Gesellschaftskreisen, eine

Internationalität, die man bei aller Mobilität heute nicht mehr antrifft.

Solch kultivierte Persönlichkeiten scheinen mit dem Ende des Ersten Weltkrieges weniger geworden zu sein und in den Zeiten dazwischen und nach dem Zweiten Weltkrieg scheint es gelungen zu sein, diese seltenen Exemplare ganz zu vernichten. Sie sind zu Romanfiguren geworden. Doch hier stand mir ein solch seltenes, kostbares Exemplar gegenüber – was für ein Geschenk!

In einer knappen Stunde führte sie mich durch ihre Geschichte – eine für mich unendliche Geschichte, und sie endet auch nie, und wird das wohl nie tun, wird stets andere Formen des Weiterlebens finden.

Im Laufe dieser Begegnung machte Maria Piscator mir klar, dass sie es ernst meinte mit dem Zusammenarbeiten, und ich willigte ein.

Eine Reise begann, mit vielen Farben und neuen Eindrücken, wie sie uns nur ein Kind oder ein ewig neugieriger Mensch bereiten kann.

Maria Ley Piscator nannte sich selbst einmal ein „Spiegelkind", welches reflektiert, eine Reflexion der ewigen Verzauberung, des ewigen Geheimnisses.

Ein Geschenk für mich, etwas von diesem Geheimnis zu entdecken, die Realität zu sehen, welche dieses Spiegelkind Maria ausmacht, das so brillant den wahren Weg ausleuchten konnte und einen ebenso wieder verspielt in die Irre führte.

Maria Piscator ist eine stete Herausforderung auf der Suche nach der Wahrheit – nach der dritten Dimension.

The Award Recipients
Die Preisträger

"Art only achieves its purpose, when it contributes to the improvement of man."

- Erwin Piscator

„Die Kunst hat nur dann Zweck, wenn sie zur Verbesserung des Menschen beiträgt."

- Erwin Piscator

1986

Lee Grant

Piscator Award, American Actress and Director, born 1927
Piscator Preis, Amerikanische Schauspielerin und Regisseurin, geboren 1927

Lee Grant made her stage debut at age four as an abducted princess in the Metropolitan Opera production of Franko Leoni's *L'Oracolo*. At age eleven, she became a member of the American Ballet, and at fourteen, she won a scholarship to New York's Neighborhood Playhouse. Sidney Kingsley recognized her talent and cast her in the ingénue role of a shoplifter for the Braodway Production of *Detective Story*.

Immediately following her successful screen debut in the same role she became a victim of the McCarthy era and was blacklisted. After twelve difficult years she resumed her career. In 1975, she received an Oscar for *Shampoo*, and was also nominated for her roles in *The Landlord* and *Voyage of the Damned*. She has directed several documentary films, including *Down and Out in America* (1986) which won the Academy Award for Documentary Feature.

In 1983, Lee Grant received the Congressional Arts Caucus Award for outstanding achievement in acting and independent film-making.

Im Alter von vier Jahren hatte Lee Grant ihr Bühnendebüt als entführte Prinzessin in Franko Leonis Oper *L'Oracolo* an der Met. Mit elf Jahren wurde sie Mitglied des American Ballet und mit 14 erhielt sie ein Stipendium für das Neighborhood Playhouse in New York. Sidney Kingsley erkannte ihr Talent und besetzte sie in der Rolle einer Ladendiebin für die Broadway Produktion *Detective Story*.

Direkt nach ihrem erfolgreichen Filmdebüt in der gleichen Rolle wurde sie ein Opfer der McCarthy Ära und auf die schwarze Liste gesetzt. Nach zwölf schwierigen Jahren konnte sie ihre Karriere fortsetzen. 1975 gewann sie einen Oscar für *Shampoo*, und wurde auch für ihre Rollen in *Der Hausbesitzer* und *Reise der Verdammten* für den Oscar nominiert. Sie hat diverse Dokumentarfilme gemacht, darunter *Down and Out in America* (1986), welcher den Oscar als bester Dokumentarfilm gewann.

1983 wurde Lee Grant mit dem Preis des Kongress-Kunstausschusses für ihre außerordentlichen Errungenschaften als Schauspielerin und Independent Filmemacherin ausgezeichnet.

1 On April 22, 1986 the American actress and director Lee Grant (left) receives the First Erwin Piscator Award from Gregorij von Leïtis (center). Actress Dolly Haas (right) toasts her colleague. She fled Germany in 1936 and in 1941 had her New York theater debut in Piscator's production of Klabund's *The Chalk Circle*

2 Prof. Dr. Volkmar Sander (left), Director of Deutsches Haus at NYU, welcomes the guests of the Erwin Piscator Award Luncheon at the National Arts Club in New York City, while Lee Grant (center) and Gregorij von Leïtis listen

3 German actress Marianne Sägebrecht (right) congratulates Lee Grant (left) on her award, while Gregorij von Leïtis looks on

4 Cecil Grace (left), who served as a member of the board of trustees of the Elysium Theater Company for several years, and his wife Booboo (center) with another guest of the First Piscator Award Luncheon

1 Am 22. April 1986 erhält die amerikanische Schauspielerin und Regisseurin Lee Grant (links) den ersten Erwin Piscator Preis von Gregorij von Leïtis (Mitte). Schauspielerin Dolly Haas (rechts), die 1936 aus Deutschland emigriert war und 1941 in Piscators Produktion von Klabunds *Kreidekreis* ihr New Yorker Theaterdebüt gab, spricht einen Toast auf ihre Kollegin aus

2 Prof. Dr. Volkmar Sander (links), Direktor des Deutschen Hauses der New York University, begrüßt die Gäste der Ersten Piscator Preisverleihung im National Arts Club in New York City, während Lee Grant (Mitte) und Gregorij von Leïtis zuhören

3 Die deutsche Schauspielerin Marianne Sägebrecht (rechts) beglückwünscht Lee Grant (links) zu ihrer Auszeichnung, während Gregorij von Leïtis zuschaut

4 Cecil Grace (links), der mehrere Jahre lang Trustee der Elysium Theater Commpany war, seine Frau Booboo (Mitte) und ein weiterer Gast des ersten Piscator Preis Luncheons

» I remember when I first saw Lee Grant at the Actors Studio. My feelings were awakened – I was so happy to feel her positive power and energy full of love and respect for the theater and the actors. I did not know much about her but from then on I knew I would want to find out more about her. She has become my mirror during this time in the United States; I started to see through her eyes the American culture and theatre world. [...] Thanks to her I saw more than before, the need for art in America that goes beyond entertainment. [...] We in Germany are more used to art being education – we expect art to do this.
But to do so in the United States, more than talent is necessary. It needs the personality of someone like Lee Grant – to fight for an idea or issue that might not be "popular", to create a situation where the audience doesn't say, "that was nice, let's go have a drink". You are forced to think about her work, you must follow up on your feelings and perhaps it doesn't change you immediately or your lifestyle, but you know there is something more behind what you have seen. «

Gregorij von Leïtis
Excerpts from his remarks on Lee Grant

» It is with gratitude and in the spirit of celebration that I have met with the Elysium and its artistic director Gregorij von Leïtis.
Some say – it's just a classical theater.
Some say – it's modern theater.
Some say – it's excellent language theater.
Some say – it's a fairy tale – "The theater of the new world."
If we have a fairy tale theater – we must have a fairy queen.
Lee Grant? [...] She is truly a gift of "the theater of the new world." Let us say, she is part of Erwin Piscator's legacy to us. «

Maria Ley Piscator
Excerpts from her remarks on Lee Grant

» Ich erinnere mich an das erste Mal, als ich Lee Grant im Actors Studio sah. Meine Gefühle waren geweckt – Ich war so froh, ihre positive Ausstrahlung und Energie zu erleben, voller Hingabe und Respekt für das Theater und die Schauspieler. Ich wusste nicht viel über sie, aber ich wusste gleich, ich wollte mehr über sie herausfinden. Sie wurde für mich zu einem Spiegel in den Vereinigten Staaten; durch Ihre Augen begann ich, die amerikanische Kultur und Theaterwelt zu betrachten. [...] Durch sie sah ich mehr als zuvor in Amerika die Notwendigkeit einer Kunst, die über bloße Unterhaltung hinausgeht. [...] In Deutschland sind wir eher gewohnt, dass Kunst Bildung bedeutet – wir erwarten von der Kunst, dass sie dies tut. Aber um dies in den Vereinigten Staaten zu erreichen, ist mehr als Talent nötig. Es braucht eine Persönlichkeit wie Lee Grant, um für eine Idee oder Sache zu kämpfen, die nicht „populär" ist, und um das Publikum dahin zu bringen, dass es nicht sagt: „Das war nett, jetzt gehen wir etwas trinken." Wenn man Lee Grant sieht, wird man gezwungen, über ihre Arbeit nachzudenken; man muß sich mit seinen eigenen Gefühlen auseinandersetzen; vielleicht ändert man sich und seinen Lebensstil nicht sofort, aber man weiß, dass mehr hinter dem steht, was man gesehen hat. «

Gregorij von Leïtis
Auszug aus seiner Laudatio auf Lee Grant

» Die Begegnung mit Elysium und seinem Intendanten Gregorij von Leïtis erfüllt mich mit Dankbarkeit und freudiger Stimmung.
Einige sagen – Elysium ist bloß ein klassisches Theater. Andere sagen – es sei modernes Theater. Wieder andere sagen – es ist hervorragendes Sprechtheater.
Einige sagen – es ist ein Märchen – „das Theater der neuen Welt." Ein Märchentheater braucht auch eine Märchenfee.
Lee Grant? [...] Sie ist wahrhaft ein Geschenk für „das Theater der neuen Welt". Sagen wir es so: Sie ist Teil des Piscatorschen Erbes für uns. «

Maria Ley Piscator
Auszug aus ihrer Laudatio auf Lee Grant

TED WEISS
17th District
New York

Chairman
Subcommittee on
Intergovernmental
Relations and
Human Resources

2442 Rayburn Building
Washington, D.C. 20515
202/225-5635

Patricia S. Fleming
Administrative Assistant

Congress of the United States
House of Representatives
April 22, 1986

Committees:

Foreign Affairs

Government Operations

Children, Youth and Families

National Commission
on Working Women

Executive Board Member,
Congressional Arts Caucus

Secretary, New York State
Congressional Delegation

CONGRESSIONAL RECORD

ELYSIUM THEATRE HONORS ACTRESS/DIRECTOR LEE GRANT

Mr. Speaker, Today at the National Arts Club, the world-renowned actress, Lee Grant, will be awarded the Erwin Piscator Award for achievement in acting, directing, and education. This ceremony will take place at a luncheon sponsored by the Elysium Theatre Company, an international repertory group located in the Congressional District which I represent.

It is particularly fitting that Ms. Grant be the recipient of this prize, because she embodies in her life and in her work, the principles that / Erwin Piscator stood for in illuminating interpersonal relationships and in relating individuals to their environment and to society.

Ms. Grant's entire life has been devoted to the performing arts having begun her career at the age of four on the stage of the Metropolitan Opera. At 14 she won a scholarship to New York's Neighborhood Playhouse which led to her Broadway debut in Detective Story, for which she was awarded the Critic Circle Award.

Hers has been a career highlighted with recognition and achievement. She is the recipient of the Best Actress Award, two Emmy Awards, and the Academy Award for Best Supporting Actress in Shampoo. In her recent career in film and stage, she has explored experiences that major studios rarely handle. In 1983 she received the Congressional Arts Caucus Award for outstanding achievement in acting and independent film-making. Her dedication, talent, and creative energy have touched the lives of everyone who has had contact with her. We are proud of her and grateful to her for having enriched our lives.

District Offices
252 7th Avenue, New York City 10001 212/620-3970   490 West 238th Street, Bronx 10463 212/884-0441
4060 Broadway, New York City 10032 212/927-7726 131 Waverly Place, New York City 10011 212/620-3310 655 East 233rd Street, Bronx 10466 212/652-0400

Bericht für das offizielle Protokoll des US-Kongresses
Kongress-Abgeordneter Ted Weiss, New York, 22. April 1986

Das Elysium Theater ehrt die Schauspielerin und Regisseurin Lee Grant.

Herr Vorsitzender, heute erhält die weltbekannte Schauspielerin Lee Grant im National Arts Club den Erwin Piscator Preis für ihre Leistungen in den Bereichen Schauspiel, Regie und Bildung. Die Preisverleihung findet statt während eines Mittagessens, das die Elysium Theater Company ausrichtet, eine internationale Repertoire-Theatergruppe, welche in dem von mir repräsentierten Kongress-Distrikt ansässig ist.

Es scheint mir in besonderer Weise angebracht, dass Frau Grant diesen Preis erhält, denn in ihrem Leben und Werk verkörpert sie die Prinzipien, von denen auch Erwin Piscator beseelt war: nämlich zwischenmenschliche Beziehungen auszuleuchten und die Beziehungen der Individuen zu ihrer Umwelt und Gesellschaft zu erhellen.

Frau Grants ganzes Leben ist den Darstellenden Künsten gewidmet, seit sie im Alter von vier Jahren ihre Karriere auf der Bühne der Metropolitan Opera begann. Mit 14 gewann sie ein Stipendium für das Neighborhood Playhouse in New York, welches in ihr Broadway-Debüt in *Detective Story* mündete, für das sie den Critic Circle Award erhielt.

Ihr beruflicher Werdegang ist von Anerkennung und Erfolg markiert. Sie hat den Best Actress Award gewonnen, zwei Emmy Auszeichnungen und den Oscar als beste Nebendarstellerin im Film *Shampoo*. In ihren jüngsten Filmen und Bühnenstücken hat sie Erfahrungswelten sondiert, die von den großen Studios selten behandelt werden. 1983 wurde sie geehrt mit dem Preis des Kongress-Kunstausschusses für ihre außerordentlichen Errungenschaften als Schauspielerin und Independent Filmemacherin.

Ihr Engagement, ihr Talent und ihre kreative Energie haben das Leben eines jeden berührt, der mit ihr in Kontakt kam. Wir sind stolz auf sie und dankbar, dass sie unser aller Leben bereichert hat.

Übersetzung: Michael Lahr

1987

Giorgio Strehler

Piscator Award, Italian Opera and Theater Director, 1921 – 1997
Piscator Preis, Italienischer Opern- und Theaterregisseur, 1921 – 1997

Giorgio Strehler made his acting debut at the Academy of Amateur Theater in Milan. During the war he was part of the resistance movement and later emigrated to Switzerland where he worked as a director in refugee camps at Mürren and Geneva.

In the spring of 1947 Strehler joined forces with Paolo Grassi and founded the Piccolo Teatro di Milano, the first permanent theater in Italy exclusively devoted to drama.

He became famous for his research and revival of the commedia dell'arte. Carlo Goldoni's long forgotten *Arlecchino: Servant of Two Masters* was one of his first productions at the Piccolo Teatro. It would become the longest running play in Italian theater. Strehler directed numerous Brecht and Shakespeare plays, but also a number of operas.

Throughout his life Strehler was faithful to his conception of a "clear and transparent" theater that can help us understand life better.

Giorgio Strehler hatte sein Schauspieldebüt an der Accademia dei Filodrammatici in Mailand. Während des Krieges schloß er sich dem Widerstand an und emigrierte später in die Schweiz. Dort war er in Mürren und Genf als Regisseur einer Exil-Theatergruppe tätig.

Im Frühjahr 1947 gründete Strehler gemeinsam mit Paolo Grassi das Piccolo Teatro di Milano, das erste ständige Sprechtheater in Italien.

Er erforschte die alte Form der commedia dell'arte und machte sie auf der Bühne wieder lebendig. Carlo Goldonis lange vergessenes Stück *Der Diener zweier Herren* war eine seiner ersten Produktionen im Piccolo Teatro. Kein anderes Stück in Italien lief solange wie dieses. Strehler inszenierte zahlreiche Brecht- und Shakespeare-Stücke, aber auch etliche Opern.

Sein Leben lang blieb Strehler seiner Idee eines „klaren und durchsichtigen" Theaters treu, welches uns helfen kann, das Leben besser zu verstehen.

1-006954A105 04/15/87 ICS IPMMOZF MTN NYAC
02381 MOORESTOWN NJ 04-15 1127A EST MOZE

GREGORIJ H VON LEITIS
97 EAST 7 ST APT 16
NEW YORK NY 10009

I HOPE YOU WILL EXPRESS TO ALL YOUR INVITED GUESTS MY DISMAY
AT HAVING TO MISS THE AWARD CEREMONY OF THE ERWIN PISCATOR AWARD
APRIL 21 IN NEW YORK. NEXT MAY 14 IN MILAN, I WILL CELEBRATE THE
40TH
COL TF2606114 97 7TH APT16 NEWYORK(10009) 21 14 MILAN, 40TH
TTY904 PAGE 2/50
ANNIVERSARY OF THE FOUNDING OF THE PICCOLO TEATRO AND I AM
ALREADY INVOLVED IN REHEARSALS OF 2 PRODUCTIONS IN MILAN.
I AM PROUD TO BE HONORED BY YOU IN THE NAME OF AN ARTIST WHOM I
CONSIDERE TO BE ONE OF MY OWN MASTERS.
CONGRATULATIONS TO YOU FOR THE WORK
COL 2
TTY904 PAGE 3/17
WHICH YOU DO TO KEEP HIS NAME
AND MEMORY PRESENT AMONGST US
WITH WARMEST GREETINGS

      GIORGIO STREHLER
      TO REPLY BY MAILGRAM MESSAGE, SEE REVERSE SIDE FOR WESTERN UNION'S TOLL - FREE PHONE NUMBERS

NEWYORK(10009)

THIS IS A CONFIRMATION COPY OF A MESSAGE ADDRESSED TO YOU

Telegramm von Giorgio Strehler an Gregorij von Leïtis
15. April 1987

Ich hoffe, Sie werden all Ihren geladenen Gästen zum Ausdruck bringen,
wie traurig ich bin, bei der Preisverleihung des Erwin Piscator Preises am
21. April nicht in New York dabei sein zu können. Am 14. Mai werde ich
in Mailand das 40jährige Gründungsjubiläum des Piccolo Teatro feiern, und
ich bin schon mitten in den Probenarbeiten für zwei Inszenierungen dort.
Ich bin stolz, von Ihnen diese Ehrung zu erhalten, die den Namen eines
Künstlers trägt, den ich selbst als einen meiner Lehrmeister betrachte.
Ich beglückwünsche Sie zu der Arbeit, die Sie leisten, um seinen Namen
und das Andenken an ihn unter uns wachzuhalten.

Mit herzlichen Grüßen,
Giorgio Strehler

1 During the second Piscator Award Luncheon on April 21, 1987 a historic re-union takes place: For the first time after several decades Maria Ley Piscator (left) meets with the US-American actress and acting teacher Stella Adler (2nd from right). In the early 1940s Stella Adler had taught at the Dramatic Workshop which Erwin Piscator had founded at the New School for Social Research. Witnessing this meeting are: Soprano Anna Moffo (right) and Gregorij von Leïtis

2 Evelyn Bausman (left), member of Elysium's board of directors, and Dr. Angelika Jansen

3 Dr. Brigitte Agstner (left), Program Director of the Austrian Cultural Forum, in conversation with the Austrian Ambassador to the UN Dr. Karl Fischer

4 Maria Ley Piscator (right) chats with other guests during the reception prior to the Award Ceremony at the National Arts Club

5 The Italian Consul General in New York, Minister Francesco Corrias (standing), praises Giorgio Strehler's merits, while Dr. Karl Fischer, Nina Raffalt, and Anna Moffo (from left) are listening. Since Giorgio Strehler couldn't be present at the Award Ceremony, Anna Moffo later accepted the award on his behalf

1 Bei der zweiten Piscator Preisverleihung am 21. April 1987 kommt es zu einer historischen Wiederbegegnung: Maria Ley Piscator (links) trifft nach mehreren Jahrzehnten erstmals wieder die US-amerikanische Schauspielerin und Schauspiellehrerin Stella Adler (2.v.r.). Stella Adler hatte Anfang der 1940er Jahre in dem von Piscator gegründeten Dramatic Workshop an der New School for Social Research unterrichtet. Mit dabei: Sopranistin Anna Moffo (rechts) und Gregorij von Leïtis (2.v.l.)

2 Evelyn Bausman (links), Mitglied des Elysium-Vorstandes, und Dr. Angelika Jansen

3 Dr. Brigitte Agstner (links), Programmdirektorin des österreichischen Kulturforums, im Gespräch mit dem österreichischen UN-Botschafter Dr. Karl Fischer

4 Maria Ley Piscator (rechts) plaudert mit anderen Gästen beim Empfang vor der Preisverleihung im National Arts Club

5 Der italienische Generalkonsul in New York Minister Francesco Corrias (stehend) würdigt die Verdienste von Giorgio Strehler, während Dr. Karl Fischer, Nina Raffalt, und Anna Moffo (v.l.n.r.) zuhören. Da Giorgio Strehler bei der Preisverleihung nicht anwesend sein kann, nimmt Anna Moffo später für ihn den Piscator Preis entgegen

1988

Judith Malina

Piscator Award, American Actress, Writer and Director, born 1926
Piscator Preis, Amerikanische Schauspielerin, Autorin und Regisseurin, geboren 1926

Born in Germany, Judith Malina emigrated to America in 1929 with her father, a rabbi, and her mother, an actress. In 1944, she began her studies as a directing student of Piscator at the Dramatic Workshop and later became his dramaturg. In 1947, she and Julian Beck founded The Living Theatre as an alternative to the commercial theater of the time.

Judith Malina's work as a director is characterized by the unique fusion of the political and aesthetic theories of Piscator and Brecht with the visceral, absolutist vision of Antonin Artaud. The uncompromising expression of her anarcho-pacifist beliefs has several times resulted in her being jailed, notably for several months in Brazil in 1971 for the creation of *The Legacy of Cain*, a cycle of street theater works protesting the military dictatorhip then in power.

Judith Malina also is the author of many essays, plays, poems, and diaries. In her study *The Piscator Notebook* (published in 2012), Malina chronicles her intensive training at Piscator's Dramatic Workshop.

In Deutschland geboren emigrierte Judith Malina 1929 mit ihrem Vater, einem Rabbiner, und ihrer Mutter, einer Schauspielerin in die USA. 1944 begann sie ihr Regie-Studium an Piscators Dramatic Workshop. Später wurde sie seine Dramaturgin. 1947 gründeten sie und Julian Beck das Living Theatre als Alternative zum kommerziellen Theater der damaligen Zeit.

Malinas Regieansatz ist geprägt durch die einzigartige Verschmelzung der politischen und ästhetischen Theorien von Piscator und Brecht mit der absoluten, die Tiefenschichten berührenden Vision eines Antonin Artaud. Die kompromisslose Bekundung ihrer anarcho-pazifistischen Überzeugung führte einige Male zu Malinas Verhaftung, so etwa 1971, als sie in Brasilien für mehrere Monate eingesperrt wurde wegen ihrer Produktion *The Legacy of Cain*, einem Straßentheater-Zyklus, der gegen die damalige Militärdiktatur aufbegehrte.

Judith Malina ist Autorin mehrerer Essays, Theaterstücke, Gedichte und Tagebücher. 2012 wurde ihr Buch *The Piscator Notebook* veröffentlicht, das ihre intensive Ausbildung an Piscators Dramatic Workshop beschreibt.

Judith Malina (standing) expresses thanks for the Third Erwin Piscator Award which she receives on April 12, 1988 at the legendary restaurant Sardi's in New York's theater district. Maria Ley Piscator, Prof. Dr. Volkmar Sander, Gregorij von Leïtis and actor BD Wong (M. Butterfly) (from left) listen attentively, while Judith Malina tells the guests, how much Erwin Piscator had shaped her as a person and an artist while she was a student at the Dramatic Workshop

Judith Malina (stehend) bedankt sich für den 3. Erwin Piscator Preis, den sie am 12. April 1988 im New Yorker Restaurant Sardi's erhält. Maria Ley Piscator, Prof. Dr. Volkmar Sander, Gregorij von Leïtis und der Schauspieler BD Wong (M. Butterfly) (v.l.n.r.) hören gespannt zu, als Judith Malina davon berichtet, wie sehr Erwin Piscator sie als Studentin des Dramatic Workshop geprägt hat

» Piscator taught me two basic things:

One was total theater, which means theater is everything and everywhere, and you can do theater on the street and in a hospital room and in an elevator. It's all theater if you make it theater. And of course this has been extended now to mean all kinds of other things that people are doing: site-specific, all the different forms of advancement that Piscator either foresaw or did. But does that mean then, that if everything is theater, nothing is theater, because it's all theater? No! It doesn't mean that. – Because, if you go to a damn theater you know that when you are standing backstage and you are talking to your fellow actor, saying "Shall we go and have a cup of coffee after the show? I still have to call …" – And you hear your cue and you walk out into the playing space, into the light, or even on the street, and you change. Because now it's theater. And you look at your fellow creature differently, you look the audience into the eye, as Piscator liked to have us do, or you look at the other actor … in a heightened way. And that's why it's theater! If everything were theater that would be very beautiful, if it meant we always behaved in a heightened form, in our highest capacity. In our most aware, cautious and daring capacity. – And that's why everything is theater – and that is total theater. That's one of the things he taught us: Total theater.

The other thing he taught us was really, that we had no right to go out into the middle of a space and say to the people around us, whether they are in a theater in the dark or whether they are sitting in a circle in an unconventional space, to say to them: "Now you be quiet. Listen to me! I have so much to tell you! Besides I am very artistic to look at, I speak beautifully, I can make you cry, I can make you laugh. Look at me! Am I not wonderful?" – This is egotistical bullshit! It doesn't belong in any art. It's sort of the opposite of art, which draws in the spectator instead of putting all the light on the performer, or the painter, or the musician. It's the music, and the painting, and the play, and the ideas. But the actor who has nothing to say, should get out of the middle, said Piscator, and let somebody speak who has something to say. Because if you are going to say: "Be quiet! Look at me," you have to have some reason to do that. Otherwise it's an absurd, authoritarian… or – because you are being paid and the audience is paying – an absurd social relationship. You have to have something you really want to say. Whether you are a stagehand or an usher, or a minor part player or the diva, or the director: You have to have something in common that you want to express. Of course that doesn't mean you can't play Adolf Hitler. Of course you can. But then you are showing what that is from the point of view of your commitment.

So Piscator taught us two things: Total theater, and commitment!

And that's certainly what The Living Theatre has striven to further explore. «

Excerpts from a conversation between Judith Malina and Michael Lahr, March 24, 2006

» Piscator lehrte uns zwei grundlegende Sachverhalte:

Das eine war das totale Theater. Das heißt: Theater ist alles und überall. Man kann Theater machen auf der Straße, in einem Krankenzimmer oder im Aufzug. Es ist alles Theater, wenn man es zum Theater macht. Natürlich ist dies inzwischen erweitert worden und bedeutet vieles mehr, was Menschen tun: ortsspezifische Performances, all die verschiedenen Formen der Weiterentwicklung, die Piscator entweder vorhersah oder selbst in die Tat umsetzte. Aber heißt das nun: Wenn alles zum Theater wird, ist nichts mehr Theater, weil alles Theater ist? Nein! Das heißt es nicht. – Denn, wenn Sie in irgendein Theater gehen und hinter der Bühne stehen und mit Ihren Schauspielkollegen sprechen und sagen: „Sollen wir nach der Vorstellung noch einen Kaffee trinken? Ich muß noch xy anrufen…" – und dann hören Sie Ihr Stichwort und gehen hinaus in die Spielstätte, ins Rampenlicht, oder auch auf die Straße, und Sie verändern sich. Denn jetzt ist es Theater. Und Sie betrachten Ihre Mitmenschen anders, Sie schauen dem Publikum in die Augen, wie Piscator es immer von uns wollte, oder Sie nehmen einen anderen Schauspieler in den Blick … in einer erhabenen Art und Weise. Aus diesem Grund ist es Theater! Wenn alles Theater wäre, wäre dies sehr schön, wenn es bedeutete, dass wir immer in einer höheren Form agieren, unser höchstes Potential verwirklichen: voll und ganz bewusst, umsichtig und wagemutig. – Deshalb ist alles Theater – und das ist das totale Theater. Das ist die eine Sache, die er uns beibrachte: Totales Theater.

Ein Zweites, was er uns lehrte, ist folgendes:

Wir haben kein Recht hinaus zu gehen mitten in einen Raum und zu den Menschen um uns herum zu sagen – ob sie nun im dunkeln Theater sitzen oder im Kreis an einem ungewöhnlichen Ort: „Jetzt seid Ihr still und hört mir zu! Ich habe so viel zu sagen. Außerdem sehe ich sehr künstlerisch aus, ich habe eine wunderbare Aussprache, ich kann Euch zum Weinen bringen und zum Lachen. Schaut mich an! Bin ich nicht großartig? – Das ist schwachsinniges Geltungsbedürfnis. Das gehört nicht in die Kunst. Es ist geradezu das Gegenteil von Kunst. Denn die Kunst zieht den Zuschauer an, und richtet nicht das Scheinwerferlicht auf den Darsteller, oder den Maler, oder den Musiker. Was zählt ist die Musik, das Bild, das Stück, die Ideen. Der Schauspieler, der nichts zu sagen hat, soll aus der Mitte verschwinden, so sagte Piscator, und denjenigen zu Wort kommen lassen, der eine Botschaft hat. Denn wenn Du sagst: „Sei still! Sieh mich an!", musst Du einen Grund dafür haben. Sonst ist es eine absurde, autoritäre … oder – weil Du bezahlt wirst und das Publikum Eintritt zahlt – eine absurde soziale Beziehung. Es muß wirklich etwas geben, was Du uns mitteilen willst. Egal, ob Du ein Bühnenarbeiter bist, oder Platzanweiser, oder eine kleine Rolle spielst, oder die Diva, oder auch der Regisseur: Ihr müsst etwas gemeinsam haben, was Ihr zum Ausdruck bringen wollt. Natürlich heißt das nicht, dass Du nicht Adolf Hitler darstellen kannst. Du kannst ihn auf die Bühne bringen. Aber dann zeigst Du, was das bedeutet aus der Perspektive Deines Bekenntnisses.

Also: Piscator lehrte uns zwei Dinge: Totales Theater und Bekenntnis!

Und genau das versuchen wir mit dem Living Theatre seither weiter zu erforschen. «

Auszüge aus einem Gespräch zwischen Judith Malina und Michael Lahr, aufgezeichnet am 24. März 2006

Peter Zadek

Piscator Award, German Theater Director and Translator, 1926 – 2009
Piscator Preis, Deutscher Theaterregisseur und Übersetzer, 1926 – 2009

Berlin-born Peter Zadek emigrated to England in 1933 with his parents who fled Nazi repression. After studying at Oxford, he enrolled at the Old-Vic-School in London. In 1957 he directed the world premiere of Jean Genet's *The Balcony* in London. The highly controversial production enraged Genet and propelled Zadek to the forefront of the theater world.

In 1958, Zadek returned to Germany. He became known for his daring, innovative interpretations and was several times chosen as "Director of the Year" by *Theater Heute* magazine. He served as Artistic Director of the Schauspielhaus Bochum, the Deutsches Schauspielhaus Hamburg and as one of five co-directors of the Berliner Ensemble.

Known in Germany as the enfant terrible of the theater, Zadek never hesitated to shock audiences, to force them to remember the past and consider the existence of a reality beyond the fringes of their complacent, affluent lives.

Der gebürtige Berliner Peter Zadek emigrierte 1933 mit seinen Eltern vor den Repressalien der Nazis nach England. Nach seinem Studium in Oxford schrieb er sich an der Old-Vic Schauspielschule in London ein. 1957 inszenierte er die Welturaufführung von Jean Genets *Der Balkon* in London. Die heftig umstrittene Produktion erboste Genet und katapultierte Zadek an die Spitze der Theaterwelt.

1958 kehrte Zadek nach Deutschland zurück. Seine mutigen, innovativen Interpretationen machten ihn berühmt; verschiedene Male wurde er vom Magazin *Theater Heute* zum „Regisseur des Jahres" gekürt. Er war Intendant des Schauspielhauses Bochum, des Deutschen Schauspielhauses Hamburg und einer von fünf Co-Direktoren des Berliner Ensembles.

In Deutschland bekannt als enfant terrible des Theaters, scheute Zadek nie davor zurück, seine Zuschauer zu schockieren, sie an die Vergangenheit zu erinnern und daran, dass es jenseits ihrer selbstgefälligen, im Überfluß schwimmenden Existenz eine andere Realität gibt.

1 American actor Al Corley (*Dynasty*), German actress and painter Jessika Cardinahl, and talent agent Robert Lantz (from right)

2 Austrian writer and actress Doris Mayer, Dr. Wolfgang Waldner, Director of the Austrian Cultural Forum, Isabell Countess Czernin, and German diplomat Dr. Peter Wittig (from left)

3 Maria-Gaetana Matisse (right) talking with Eckbert von Bohlen und Halbach

4 Uschi Grüterich (left) and Werner Walbroel, President of the German-American Chamber of Commerce in New York, at the Fourth Piscator Award Luncheon on April 11, 1989 at "Sardi's

1 US-Schauspieler Al Corley (*Der Denver-Clan*), die deutsche Schauspielerin und Malerin Jessika Cardinahl und der Künstleragent Robert Lantz (v.r.n.l.)

2 Die österreichische Schriftstellerin und Schauspielerin Doris Mayer, der Direktor des österreichischen Kulturforums Dr. Wolfgang Waldner, Isabell Gräfin von Czernin und der deutsche Diplomat Dr. Peter Wittig (v.l.n.r.)

3 Maria-Gaetana Matisse (rechts) im Gespräch mit Eckbert von Bohlen und Halbach

4 Uschi Grüterich (links) und Werner Walbroel, Chef der Deutsch-Amerikanischen Handelskammer in New York, beim 4. Piscator Luncheon am 11. April 1989 im „Sardi's"

5 Maria Ley Piscator (left) with German filmmaker Katharina Otto-Bernstein (right), and Dieter von Lehsten (2nd from right). In the background: Arnet Beyer

6 Austrian dramatist Bernhard Schärfl, Kicki von Bohlen und Halbach, Gesa-Christine Vergau, and Gregorij von Leïtis (from right) listen …

7 … while Dr. Jo-Jacqueline Eckardt speaks about Peter Zadek

5 Maria Ley Piscator (links) mit der deutschen Filmemacherin Katharina Otto-Bernstein (rechts) und Dieter von Lehsten (2.v.r.). Im Hintergrund: Arnet Beyer

6 Der österreichische Dramatiker Bernhard Schärfl, Kicki von Bohlen und Halbach, Gesa-Christine Vergau und Gregorij von Leïtis (v.r.n.l.) lauschen gespannt,…

7 … während Dr. Jo-Jacqueline Eckardt die Laudatio auf Peter Zadek hält

1990

Robert Wilson

Piscator Award, American Director, Playwright, Painter, and Video Artist, born 1941
Piscator Preis, Amerikanischer Regisseur, Dramatiker, Maler und Videokünstler, geboren 1941

A native of Waco, Texas, Robert Wilson graduated from Brooklyn's Pratt Institute in 1965. Since his first signature works, including *Deafman Glance* and *The Life and Times of Joseph Stalin*, he has been at the forefront of innovative international theater. His monumental opera *Einstein on the Beach*, created with composer Philip Glass achieved worldwide acclaim.

Wilson has worked with major European theaters and opera houses and collaborated with an array of internationally known artists, including Heiner Müller, Allen Ginsberg, Lou Reed, and Marina Abramovic.

Wilson's works are known for their austere style and very slow movement.

Wilson's drawings, furniture designs and installations have been exhibited in museums and galleries worldwide.

Each summer he invites students and experienced professionals to the Watermill Center, a laboratory for the arts and humanities on Long Island.

Der aus Waco, Texas stammende Robert Wilson machte 1965 seinen Abschluß am Pratt Institute in Brooklyn. Seine ersten charakteristischen Arbeiten *Deafman Glance* und *The Life and Times of Joseph Stalin* etablierten seinen Ruf in der internationalen Theaterwelt. Seine monumentale Oper *Einstein on the Beach*, die er mit dem Komponisten Philip Glass schuf, wurde weltweit bejubelt.

Wilson hat an den führenden europäischen Theatern und Opernhäusern gearbeitet und kooperiert mit einer Vielzahl international bekannter Künstler, darunter Heiner Müller, Allen Ginsberg, Lou Reed und Marina Abramovic. Wilsons Produktionen zeichnen sich aus durch ihren strengen Stil und ihre sehr langsamen Bewegungen.

Wilsons Zeichnungen, Möbelentwürfe und Installationen sind in Museen und Galerien weltweit zu sehen.

Jeden Sommer lädt er Studenten und erfahrene Fachleute ein in sein Watermill Center, ein Laboratorium für die Künste und Geisteswissenschaften auf Long Island.

1 Mary Sharp Cronson, honoree Robert Wilson, Dieter von Lehsten and Isabell Countess Czernin (from left) at the Piscator Award Ceremony on April 12, 1990 at Sardi's in New York City

2 Avant-garde artist Robert Wilson with Maria Ley Piscator and Gregorij von Leïtis (from right)

3 Maria Ley Piscator (2nd from right) in lively conversation with members of the Elysium Ensemble

1 Mary Sharp Cronson, Preisträger Robert Wilson, Dieter von Lehsten und Isabell Gräfin von Czernin (v.l.n.r.) vor der Preisverleihungszeremonie am 12. April 1990 im Sardi's-Restaurant in New York City

2 Der Avantgarde-Künstler Robert Wilson mit Maria Ley Piscator und Gregorij von Leïtis (v.r.n.l.)

3 Maria Ley Piscator (2.v.r.) unterhält sich angeregt mit Mitgliedern des Elysium Ensembles

» Erwin Piscator had a strong vision of Art: He believed that theatre – at its finest – possesses a therapeutic power that can create positive change for a better world.

Robert Wilson's early work included therapeutic dance and movement workshops with what were considered "subnormal", hyperactive and braindamaged individuals. Theater was born from these experiences, including pieces by paraplegics and "ballet" for bed-bound iron-lung patients. *Deafman Glance*, an instant hit in 1970, was inspired from insights given him by a teenage deafmute. If there was a message, it was – and I quote – that "difference was to be prized, stimulated and encouraged, not suppressed in a fallacious process of 'normalization'."[1]

Robert Wilson's theater, like that of Piscator's is a dialectic between individual freedom and mechanization. It is a theater rich in details – down to the smallest gesture. And the dialogue is not the major part of the performance, but another tip of the iceberg.

I tell my actors at the Elysium Theater Company that the text is like the whipped cream of the performance. We do not tell the audience what to think, feel and see – that is a limited art. Our work is to find the gesture. The importance of the gesture is seen constantly in Robert Wilson's work. «

Gregorij von Leïtis
Excerpts from his remarks on Robert Wilson

» Erwin Piscator hatte eine starke künstlerische Vision. Er glaubte, dass Theater – in seiner besten Form – therapeutische Kraft besitzt, die eine Veränderung hin zu einer besseren Welt hervorbringen kann.

Robert Wilsons frühe Arbeit beinhaltete therapeutische Tanz- und Bewegungs-Workshops mit sog. „subnormalen", hyperaktiven und hirngeschädigten Individuen. Wilsons Theater wurde geboren aus diesen Erfahrungen, sowie aus Stücken mit Querschnittgelähmten und „Ballett" für bettlägrige Patienten mit Beatmungsgerät. *Deafman Glance*, 1970 sofort ein Erfolg, war inspiriert von den Erfahrungen eines jugendlichen Taubstummen. Die darin vermittelte Botschaft war – ich zitiere, dass „Verschiedenheit geschätzt, gefördert und gestärkt werden soll, nicht unterdrückt in einem trügerischen Prozeß der ‚Normalisierung'."[1]

Robert Wilsons Theater, wie das von Piscator, besteht in einer Dialektik zwischen persönlicher Freiheit und Mechanisierung. Es ist ein Theater reich an Details – bis hin zur kleinsten Geste. Und der Dialog ist nicht der entscheidende Teil der Vorstellung, sondern die Spitze eines Eisberges.

Ich sage meinen Schauspielern in der Elysium Theater Company immer, dass der Text die Sahnehaube auf der Vorstellung ist. Wir sagen dem Publikum nicht, was es denken, fühlen und sehen soll – das ist eine begrenzte Form von Kunst. Unsere Arbeit besteht darin, die Geste zu finden. Wie wichtig die Geste ist, kann man ständig in Robert Wilsons Arbeit erkennen. «

Gregorij von Leïtis
Auszug aus seiner Laudatio auf Robert Wilson

1. Director's Theatre by David Bradby and David Williams, published by Macmillan, 1968

1993

Klaus-Dieter Wilke

Piscator Award, German Director, born 1944
Piscator Preis, Deutscher Regisseur, geboren 1944

Klaus-Dieter Wilke studied art history, philosophy, drama and German philology in Cologne, Germany, and later in Vienna, Austria. In 1965, he attended the Max-Reinhardt-Seminar.

In 1966 he became assistant director at the Bregenzer Festspiele, later that same year he joined the Vienna Burgtheater staff, where he worked until 1972. His directing career began with his production of Schnitzler's *Flirtation* in 1971. Until 1976 he worked as a free-lance director in Germany, Austria, and Switzerland.

In 1977, Klaus-Dieter Wilke became director at the State Theater Linz in Austria. In 1981, he started work as artistic and personal assistant to the managing director in Bregenz. Thanks to him the Bregenzer Festspiele achieved a higher artistic level, and with a new variety of performances a much greater public attractiveness. In 1984, he returned to the State Theater Linz. He now again works as a free-lance director. One of his latest projects is *The Kick*, a play and accompanying workshop against juvenile violence.

Klaus-Dieter Wilke studierte Kunstgeschichte, Philosophie, Theater und Germanistik in Köln und später in Wien. 1965 besuchte er das Max-Reinhardt-Seminar.

1966 wurde er Regieassistent bei den Bregenzer Festspielen. Noch im gleichen Jahr wechselte er ans Burgtheater, wo er bis 1972 arbeitete. Seine Laufbahn als Regisseur begann 1971 mit seiner Inszenierung von Schnitzlers *Liebelei*. Bis 1976 arbeitete er als freischaffender Regisseur in Deutschland, Österreich und der Schweiz.

1977 wurde er als Regisseur ans Landestheater Linz engagiert. 1981 wechselte er als Leiter des Betriebsbüros, persönlicher Referent und Stellvertreter des Direktors in künstlerischen Fragen nach Bregenz. Er rief die Aktion „Jugend und Festspiele" ins Leben und gab alternativen Bestrebungen Raum. Seiner Mithilfe ist es zu verdanken, dass die Bregenzer Festspiele seither große Beachtung finden. 1984 kehrte er nach Linz zurück. Heute ist er wieder freischaffend tätig. Eines seiner jüngsten Projekte ist *Der Kick*, ein Stück mit begleitenden Workshops gegen Jugendgewalt.

1994

William M. Hoffman

Piscator Award, American Playwright, Editor, and Educator, born 1939
Piscator Preis, Amerikanischer Dramatiker, Herausgeber und Lehrer, geboren 1939

William M. Hoffman wrote the libretto to the opera *The Ghosts of Versailles* (music: John Corigliano) which premiered at the Metropolitan Opera in 1991. Two years later it received the first International Classical Music award as best new musical event of the year.

Hoffman is also the author of *As Is*, one of the first plays to focus on AIDS. Its Broadway production in 1985 earned him a Drama Desk Award, an Obie, as well as a Tony nomination for best play. Since then *As Is* has received innumerable productions and has been seen in over fifteen foreign countries.

A native New Yorker, Hoffman started writing at New York's legendary Caffe Cino and La Mama. Among his plays are *A Book of Etiquette*, *The Cherry Orchard / Part II*, *Cornbury* (with Anthony Holland), and *Shoe Palace Murray*. He is also known for his translations, which include Euripides' *Iphigenia in Aulis* and Aeschylus' *Orestia*.

The editor of four drama anthologies, he is currently Professor of Theater at Lehman College at the City University of New York.

William M. Hoffman schrieb das Libretto zur Oper *The Ghosts of Versailles* (Musik: John Corigliano), die 1991 an der Met uraufgeführt wurde. Zwei Jahre später erhielt die Oper den 1. Internationalen Klassischen Musikpreis als bestes neues Musikereignis des Jahres.

Hoffman schrieb auch *Wie Du*, eines der ersten Stücke über AIDS. Die Broadway-Inszenierung 1985 trug ihm einen Drama Desk Award, einen Obie und die Tony Nominierung als bestes Stück ein. Seither wurde *Wie Du* unzählige Male aufgeführt und in über 15 Ländern gespielt.

Der gebürtige New Yorker begann seine Karriere im legendären Caffe Cino und bei La Mama. Zu seinen Stücken zählen: *A Book of Etiquette*, *The Cherry Orchard, Part II*, *Cornbury* (mit Anthony Holland) und *Shoe Palace Murray*. Auch als Übersetzer hat er sich hervorgetan, etwa mit Euripides' *Iphigenia in Aulis* und mit Aischylus' *Orestia*.

Der Herausgeber von vier Dramen-Bänden ist Professor für Theater am Lehman College der City University New York.

1995

Prof. Dr. Margret Herzfeld-Sander

Piscator Award, German Professor and Educator, born 1924
Piscator Preis, Deutsche Professorin und Lehrerin, geboren 1924

Margret Herzfeld-Sander was a faculty member of NYU for over 30 years. Her writings and research mainly focussed on the drama of the 19th and 20th century, the European realist novel, and Frankfurt School Theory. At Deutsches Haus she regularly introduced the stage readings of contemporary German-speaking playwrights organized by Elysium. She has worked tirelessly to foster German-American cultural understanding.

Margret Herzfeld-Sander gehörte über 30 Jahre dem Lehrkörper der New York University an. Sie widmete sich hauptsächlich dem Drama des 19. und 20. Jahrhunderts, dem realistischen europäischen Roman und der Frankfurter Schule. Im Deutschen Haus der NYU führte sie regelmäßig in die von Elysium veranstalteten dramatischen Lesungen zeitgenössischer deutschsprachiger Autoren ein. Sie engagierte sich unermüdlich für den deutsch-amerikanischen Kulturaustausch.

Prof. Dr. Volkmar Sander

Piscator Award, German Professor, Editor and Founder of Deutsches Haus at NYU, 1929 – 2011
Piscator Preis, Deutscher Professor, Herausgeber und Gründer des Deutschen Hauses der NYU, 1929 – 2011

Volkmar Sander was Professor of German at NYU from 1963 until 1995, serving many years as Chair of the German faculty. After years of vigorous fundraising, he founded Deutsches Haus at NYU in 1977. Thanks to him Deutsches Haus established itself as a meeting point of German-American exchange. The author of numerous books, Sander also was General Editor of the *German Library*, a 100-volume series of German thought in translation.

Volkmar Sander war von 1963 bis 1995 Professor für Germanistik an der NYU, und viele Jahre Ordinarius der deutschen Fakultät. Nach jahrelangem intensivem Fundraising gründete er 1977 das Deutsche Haus der NYU. Unter seiner Leitung wurde das Deutsche Haus ein wichtiger deutsch-amerikanischer Treffpunkt. Sander ist Autor zahlreicher Bücher und war Herausgeber der *German Library*, einer auf 100 Bände angelegten Serie deutschen Gedankengutes in Übersetzung.

1 Christine Schurtman (left), who for more than two decades has been volunteering as translator and English language consultant for Elysium, with Ulrike von Lehsten on April 18, 1995 at the Piscator Award Ceremony at Deutsches Haus at New York University

2 Prof. Dr. Friedrich Ulfers (right) congratulates Prof. Dr. Margret Herzfeld-Sander (left) on her Piscator Award

3 Dr. Heidrun Suhr, Prof. Dr. Barbara Elling, who spoke about Prof. Dr. Volkmar Sander, and Gregorij von Leïtis (from left)

1 Christine Schurtman (links), die seit mehr als zwei Jahrzehnten ehrenamtlich als Übersetzerin für Elysium tätig ist, mit Ulrike von Lehsten am 18. April 1995 bei der Piscator Preisverleihung im Deutschen Haus der New York University

2 Prof. Dr. Friedrich Ulfers (rechts) gratuliert Prof. Dr. Margret Herzfeld-Sander (links) zum Piscator Preis

3 Dr. Heidrun Suhr, Prof. Dr. Barbara Elling, welche die Laudatio auf Prof. Dr. Volkmar Sander hielt, und Gregorij von Leïtis (v.l.n.r.)

» As we remember Piscator today, we honor a member of the academy in his name, someone, who understands that a firm anchoring in the host culture is essential for any building of cultural bridges. And so he built the house in which we are gathered tonight. And he made it part of one of the important American universities. [...]
We honor Volkmar Sander, who did all this while building and administering a university German department for 28 years, while teaching and guiding generations of students, and while publishing, editing and overseeing three series of publications. [...]

By example he taught us, that it is possible to be both idealistic and pragmatic without having to compromise. By that I mean that Volkmar was never interested in power or influence for their own sake, but used, whatever he had gained of either, very skilfully here and in Germany for totally unselfish ends – es ging ihm immer um die Sache – for his cause and missions, all designed to insure German culture a greater presence in this city and this country. [...]

Volkmar was never a Germanist in the strict sense of the word – one focused on one author, one period, one critical theory or one motif, writing about these in convoluted German prose. Volkmar's training, teaching and publishing crossed disciplinary lines long before it became fashionable. «

Prof. Dr. Barbara Elling
Excerpts from her remarks on Prof. Dr. Volkmar Sander

» Während wir heute an Piscator erinnern, ehren wir in seinem Namen ein Mitglied der akademischen Welt, jemanden, der weiß, dass das feste Verankert-Sein in der Gastkultur entscheidend ist für jede Form kulturellen Brückenbaus. Und so baute er das Haus, in dem wir heute Abend versammelt sind. Und er machte es zum Bestandteil einer der wichtigsten amerikanischen Universitäten. [...]

Wir ehren Volkmar Sander, der dies alles schuf, während er 28 Jahre lang die germanistische Fakultät aufbaute und verwaltete, lehrte, Generationen von Studenten betreute, schrieb, publizierte und die Herausgabe dreier Buchserien managte.

Durch sein Beispiel lehrte er uns, dass es möglich ist, gleichzeitig idealistisch und pragmatisch zu sein, ohne Kompromisse schließen zu müssen. Ich meine damit, dass Volkmar nie an Macht oder Einfluß um ihrer selbst willen interessiert war, sondern beides sehr geschickt hier und in Deutschland nutzte für ganz selbstlose Zwecke – es ging ihm immer um die Sache – für sein Ziel, immer darum bemüht, der deutschen Kultur eine größere Plattform in dieser Stadt und diesem Land zu schaffen. [...]

Volkmar war nie ein Germanist im strengen Sinne des Wortes – jemand, der sich auf einen Autor, eine Epoche, eine Kritische Theorie oder ein Motiv konzentriert und darüber in verschachteltem Deutsch schreibt. Volkmars Ausbildung, Lehre und publizistische Tätigkeit überschritt fachliche Grenzen, lange bevor dies Mode wurde. «

Prof. Dr. Barbara Elling
Auszug aus ihrer Laudatio auf Prof. Dr. Volkmar Sander

Marshall W. Mason

Piscator Award, American Director, and Co-Founder of Circle Repertory Company, born 1940
Piscator Preis, Amerikanischer Regisseur und Mitbegründer der Circle Repertory Company, geboren 1940

Marshall W. Mason studied with Harold Clurman and Lee Strasberg at the Actors Studio. He was the co-founder and for 18 years artistic director of the Circle Repertory Company in New York. While working with the Circle Repertory Company, he discovered and nurtured many new playwrights and actors.

In 1965 he directed *Balm in Gilead* by Lanford Wilson. Since then he has directed more than sixty productions of Wilson's plays, among them *Redwood Curtain*, *Angels Fall*, and *Talley's Folly*. Off-Broadway Marshall Mason was awarded five Obies, one for the New York premiere of Tennessee Williams' *Battle of Angels*. He has worked in regional theaters throughout the United States, and also directed in London and Tokyo, where he staged *Who's Afraid of Virginia Woolf?*

Mason is Professor Emeritus of Theater at Arizona State University and the author of the book *Creating Life on Stage: A Director's Approach to Working with Actors.*

Marshall W. Mason studierte mit Harold Clurman und Lee Strasberg am Actors Studio. Er ist Mitbegründer und war 18 Jahre lang Intendant der Circle Repertory Company in New York. Während dieser Zeit entdeckte und förderte er viele junge Dramatiker und Schauspieler.

1965 führte er Regie in *Balm in Gilead* von Lanford Wilson. Seither hat er über 60 Produktionen von Wilsons Stücken inszeniert, darunter *Redwood Curtain*, *Angels Fall* und *Talley's Folly*. Off-Broadway wurde Mason fünfmal mit dem Obie ausgezeichnet, u.a. für seine New Yorker Erstaufführung von Tennessee Williams' Stück *Battle of Angels*. Er hat an vielen regionalen Theatern in den USA gearbeitet und auch in London und Tokyo, wo er *Wer hat Angst vor Virginia Woolf?* inszenierte.

Mason ist emeritierter Professor für Theater an der Arizona State University und Autor des Buches *Creating Life on Stage: A Director's Approach to Working with Actors.*

Lucille Lortel

Honorary Piscator Award, American Producer and Artistic Director, 1900 – 1999
Piscator Ehrenpreis, Amerikanische Produzentin und Intendantin, 1900 – 1999

Lucille Lortel is well known as the "Queen of Off-Broadway". She was Founder and Artistic Director of the White Barn Theatre in Westport, Connecticut, established in 1947 to present works of an unusual and experimental nature. At the White Barn Theatre she premiered such plays as Ionesco's *The Chairs*, Albee's *Fam and Yam*, and Beckett's *Embers*.

In 1955, her husband Louis Schweitzer presented Lucille Lortel with the Theatre de Lys in New York City's Greenwich Village. She opened her new theatre, which later would be called the Lucille Lortel Theatre, with *The Threepenny Opera* by Kurt Weill and Bertolt Brecht, in the translation of Marc Blitzstein. It ran for seven years.

As artistic director of the ANTA (American National Theatre and Academy) Matinee Series, from its inception in 1956, Lucille Lortel fostered many Off-Broadway successes.

A landmark of Off-Broadway, the Lucille Lortel Theatre continues to this day and is now exclusively open for Not-for-Profit-productions.

Lucille Lortel gilt als „Königin des Off-Broadway". Sie war Gründerin und Intendantin des White Barn Theaters in Westport, Connecticut, das 1947 seine Türen öffnete mit dem Ziel, Stücke von ungewöhnlicher und experimenteller Natur zu zeigen. Sie führte dort etwa Ionescos *Die Stühle*, Albees *Fam and Yam* und Becketts *Aschenglut* auf.

1955 schenkte ihr Mann Louis Schweitzer Lucille Lortel das Theatre de Lys in New Yorks Stadtteil Greenwich Village. Sie eröffnete ihr neues Theater, welches später nach ihr benannt wurde, mit Kurt Weills und Bertolt Brechts *Dreigroschenoper* in der Übersetzung von Marc Blitzstein. Das Stück lief für sieben Jahre.

Als Künstlerische Leiterin der ANTA (American National Theatre and Academy) Matinee-Serie, präsentierte sie unzählige Stücke, von denen viele später am Off-Broadway Erfolg hatten.

Das Lucille Lortel Theater, eine Institution des Off-Broadway, arbeitet bis heute weiter und steht nun ausschließlich gemeinnützigen Theaterproduktionen offen.

THE CITY OF NEW YORK
OFFICE OF THE MAYOR
NEW YORK, N.Y. 10007

March 20, 1996

Dear Friends:

It gives me great pleasure to send greetings to those attending the Ninth Annual Erwin Piscator Award Ceremony hosted by Elysium - Between Two Continents. This is a special occasion as you commemorate past achievements and prepare for future challenges.

On behalf of the residents of New York City, I commend tonight's honorees Lucille Lortel and Marshall W. Mason for their contributions to the community. Moreover, I commend those associated with Elysium - Between Two Continents for their efforts to foster cultural exchange between Europe and America and for their commitment to bringing people together through performance, theater and music. It is always gratifying to unite with those who contribute so much to the community.

Please accept my best wishes for an enjoyable ceremony and for continued success in all of your future endeavors.

Sincerely,

Rudolph W. Giuliani
Mayor

Grußbotschaft des New Yorker Bürgermeisters
Rudolph W. Giuliani, New York, 20. März 1996

Liebe Freunde,

es ist mir eine große Freude, Ihnen allen Grüße zu senden, die Sie der von Elysium – between two continents veranstalteten Neunten Jährlichen Erwin Piscator Preisverleihung beiwohnen. Dies ist eine besondere Gelegenheit, da Sie an vergangene Leistungen erinnern und sich auf zukünftige Herausforderungen vorbereiten.

Im Namen der Bürger von New York City spreche ich den heutigen Preisträgern Lucille Lortel und Marshall W. Mason Dank und Respekt aus für ihre Beiträge zum Gemeinwesen. Außerdem möchte ich allen, die mit Elysium – between two continents verbunden sind, danken für ihre Bemühungen, den kulturellen Austausch zwischen Europa und Amerika zu unterstützen und für ihren Einsatz, Menschen durch künstlerische Darbietungen, Theater und Musik zusammen zu bringen. Es ist immer erfreulich, sich mit denen zu verbinden, die so viel zum Gemeinwohl beisteuern.

Ich sende meine besten Wünsche für eine erfreuliche Zeremonie und für den weiteren Erfolg all Ihrer zukünftigen Vorhaben.

Mit freundlichen Grüßen,

Rudolph W. Giuliani
Bürgermeister

1 Marshall W. Mason (right) and Gregorij von Leïtis (left) applaud Lucille Lortel (center), recipient of the first Honorary Erwin Piscator Award in memory of Maria Ley Piscator

2 Annegret Decker (left), who served as mistress of ceremonies at the Piscator Award on March 20, 1996 at the National Arts Club, and Marshall W. Mason, Piscator Award recipient of 1996, present Lucille Lortel with flowers

3 Lucille Lortel, the "Queen of Off-Broadway"

1 Marshall W. Mason (rechts) und Gregorij von Leïtis (links) applaudieren Lucille Lortel (Mitte), der Preisträgerin des ersten Erwin Piscator Ehrenpreises in Erinnerung an Maria Ley Piscator

2 Annegret Decker (links), die die Preisverleihungszeremonie am 20. März 1996 im National Arts Club moderierte, und der Erwin Piscator Preisträger 1996, Marshall W. Mason (rechts), überreichen Lucille Lortel Blumen

3 Die „Königin des Off-Broadway" Lucille Lortel

Übersetzung: Michael Lahr

Lanford Wilson

Piscator Award, American Playwright, 1937 – 2011
Piscator Preis, Amerikanischer Dramatiker, 1937 – 2011

Lanford Wilson helped to advance the Off-Off-Broadway theater movement. His play *The Madness of Lady Bright*, dealing with a neurotic aging drag queen, premiered at Caffe Cino in 1964 and was the venue's first significant success. In 1969 he co-founded the Circle Repertory Company with Marshall W. Mason and others. Many of his plays were first presented there.

Gay identity is a major theme in Wilson's work: *Lemon Sky*, *Fifth of July*, and *Burn This* all deal with sexual identity. Ben Brantley, theatre critic of the New York Times, wrote that Wilson's plays reflect "disenchantment with the state of the nation."

In addition to writing theatre plays, Wilson wrote the libretti for several new operas, collaborating with composer Lee Hoiby.

In 1980, he received the Pulitzer Prize for Drama, in 2001 he was inducted into the Theater Hall of Fame, and in 2004 he was elected to the American Academy of Arts and Letters.

Lanford Wilson lieferte wichtige Anstöße für die Off-Off-Broadway Theaterbewegung. Sein Stück *The Madness of Lady Bright*, das von einem neurotischen alternden Transvestiten handelt, wurde 1964 im Caffe Cino aufgeführt und war der erste bedeutende Erfolg dieser Spielstätte. 1969 gründete er zusammen mit Marshall W. Mason und anderen die Circle Repertory Company. Viele seiner Stücke wurden dort zuerst gezeigt.

Homosexuelle Identität ist Hauptthema in vielen seiner Stücke: *Lemon Sky*, *Fifth of July*, und *Burn This* befassen sich alle damit. Ben Brantley, Theaterkritiker der New York Times, schrieb, dass Wilsons Stücke „Ernüchterung über den Zustand der Nation" widerspiegeln.

Neben Theaterstücken hat Wilson die Libretti für einige neue Opern in Zusammenarbeit mit dem Komponisten Lee Hoiby geschrieben.

1980 gewann er den Pulitzer Preis für Drama, 2001 wurde er in die Theater Hall of Fame aufgenommen, 2004 zum Mitglied der Amerikanischen Akademie für Kunst und Wissenschaft gewählt.

Prof. Gabriele Henkel

Honorary Piscator Award, German Artist, Writer, Art Collector, and Philanthropist
Piscator Ehrenpreis, Deutsche Künstlerin, Autorin, Kunstsammlerin und Mäzenin

Gabriele Henkel created the renowned art collection of the Henkel Company in Düsseldorf, Germany. At the beginning of the 1970s she started collecting sculptures, paintings, photographs and textiles all over the world, including works by George Rickey, Frank Stella, Seydou Keïta, and Imi Knoebel.

As a philanthropist she has supported the talents of many artists. In 2001 she established the Kythera Kulturstiftung (Kythera Cultural Foundation) which annually presents the Kythera Prize to artists who have fostered the cultural exchange between Germany and the Romance countries.

Gabriele Henkel is an artist and writer in her own right: She has published several books, including *Tafelbilder (Panel Paintings)*, *Les Beaux Restes*, and *Augenblicke (Moments)*. Notable exhibitions of her own works include: the installation *Denk ich an Heine (When I think of Heine)* at the West-German Art Fair, and *Col Lume d'un sorriso – Fragments of Longing* in Potsdam. Since 1983 she has been teaching communication design at the University of Wuppertal, Germany.

Gabriele Henkel baute die berühmte Kunstsammlung der Firma Henkel in Düsseldorf auf. Anfang der 70er Jahre begann sie, Skulpturen, Bilder, Photographien und Textilien aus aller Welt zu sammeln, darunter Werke von George Rickey, Frank Stella, Seydou Keïta und Imi Knoebel.

Als Mäzenin hat sie die Talente vieler Künstler gefördert. 2001 gründete sie die Kythera Kulturstiftung, die jährlich den Kythera Preis verleiht an Künstler, die sich Verdienste um den Kulturaustausch zwischen Deutschland und den romanischen Ländern erworben haben.

Gabriele Henkel ist selbst Künstlerin und Autorin. Sie hat diverse Bücher veröffentlicht, darunter *Tafelbilder*, *Les Beaux Restes – Bilder der Vergänglichkeit*, und *Augenblicke – Interviews, Reviews, Views*. Ihre eigenen Arbeiten wurden in verschiedenen Ausstellungen gezeigt, etwa *Denk ich an Heine* bei der Westdeutschen Kunstmesse oder *Col Lume d'un sorriso – Fragmente der Sehnsucht* in Potsdam. Als Honorarprofessorin lehrt sie Kommunikationsdesign an der Bergischen Universität Wuppertal.

1 Actress and acting teacher Helen von Münchhofen (center) with the set designer Edgar Schreiner (left) and his wife

2 Olaf Unsoeld, Eva-Maria Nerlich and Michael Lahr (from right)

3 Sabine Gewinner-Thomson (left), who for many years was an actress in the Elysium ensemble, talks with Claudia Steinberg

4 The German Consul General Dr. Cornel Metternich (center) and his wife Hilary with Dr. Stephan Nobbe, Director of the Goethe Institut New York

5 Dorrit Wohl (left), Deputy Cultural Commissioner of New York City, who conveyed a message of greeting from Mayor Rudolph W. Giuliani, with Michael Lahr (center) and Gregorij von Leïtis

1 Schauspielerin und Schauspiellehrerin Helen von Münchhofen (Mitte) mit dem Bühnenbildner Edgar Schreiner (links) und dessen Frau

2 Olaf Unsoeld, Eva-Maria Nerlich und Michael Lahr (v.r.n.l.)

3 Sabine Gewinner-Thomson (links), die viele Jahre lang Schauspielerin im Elysium-Ensemble war, im Gespräch mit Claudia Steinberg

4 Der deutsche Generalkonsul Dr. Cornel Metternich (Mitte) und dessen Frau Hilary mit Dr. Stephan Nobbe, Direktor des Goethe Instituts New York

5 Dorrit Wohl (links), die als stellvertretende Kulturdezernentin der Stadt New York eine Grußbotschaft von Bürgermeister Rudolph W. Giuliani überbrachte, mit Michael Lahr (Mitte) und Gregorij von Leïtis

6 Hilde Hlawatsch studies the program of the award ceremony

7 Margotte Marquesa de Lyon, Christa Percopo, Dr. Christoph Sturm and his mother Renate Sturm (from left) at the reception following the award ceremony

8 George Prince of Serbia

9 Dramatist Lanford Wilson (left) and the Austrian Consul General Dr. Walter Greinert prior to the award ceremony on March 20, 1997 at the Goethe Institut New York

6 Hilde Hlawatsch studiert das Programm der Preisverleihung

7 Margotte Marquesa de Lyon, Christa Percopo, Dr. Christoph Sturm und dessen Mutter Renate Sturm (v.l.n.r.) beim anschließenden Empfang

8 Georg Prinz von Serbien

9 Dramatiker Lanford Wilson (links) vor der Preisverleihung am 20. März 1997 im Goethe Institut New York mit dem österreichischen Generalkonsul Dr. Walter Greinert

BUNDESREPUBLIK DEUTSCHLAND
DER BUNDESKANZLER

Bonn, den 10. März 1997

Grußwort

Allen Teilnehmern am Festakt zur Verleihung des Erwin-Piscator-Preises im Goethe Institut zu New York übermittle ich meine herzlichen Grüße und guten Wünsche.

Ich gratuliere dem diesjährigen Träger des Preises, Herrn Lanford Wilson, und der Trägerin des Ehrenpreises, Frau Professor Gabriele Henkel. Jeder von Ihnen beiden hat einen herausragenden Beitrag zum kulturellen Reichtum der eigenen Nation und zu einem lebendigen Kulturaustausch über den Atlantik hinweg geleistet. Ich bin gewiß, daß Sie in den Ihnen verliehenen Preisen nicht nur Zeichen der Anerkennung und des Dankes, sondern auch einen Ansporn für Ihr künftiges Wirken sehen. Dazu wünsche ich Ihnen viel Erfolg.

Gerne benutze ich diese Gelegenheit, um auch „Elysium Between Two Continents" meine Anerkennung auszudrücken für das langjährige, nachhaltig wirksame Engagement, mit dem es an der konkreten Ausgestaltung der kulturellen Beziehungen Amerikas zu Europa und insbesondere zu Deutschland mitgewirkt hat. Mit Freude habe ich zur Kenntnis genommen, wie fruchtbar und erfolgreich dabei die Zusammenarbeit mit den deutschen kulturellen Mittlerorganisationen und den diplomatischen und konsularischen Vertretungen Deutschlands gewesen ist.

Ich hoffe, daß alle, denen ein lebhafter transatlantischer Kulturaustausch am Herzen liegt, diese Preisverleihung als Ermutigung empfinden.

Mit freundlichen Grüßen

Message of the Chancellor of the Federal Republic of Germany
Helmut Kohl, Bonn, March 10, 1997

I send my kindest regards and best wishes to all the guests of the Erwin Piscator Award Ceremony at the Goethe Institut in New York.

I commend this year's Award recipient, Mr. Lanford Wilson, and the Honorary Award recipient, Prof. Gabriele Henkel. Both of you have made an extraordinary contribution to the cultural enrichment of your own nation and to a vital cultural exchange across the Atlantic. I am sure, that you take this award not only as a sign of appreciation and gratitude, but also as a stimulus for your future activities. With these I wish you a lot of success.

I happily use this occasion to express my acknowledgment towards Elysium – between two continents for its long and effective engagement, with which it has contributed to the concrete shaping of cultural relations between America and Europe, especially Germany. With pleasure I noticed how productive and successful the cooperation with the German cultural organizations and the diplomatic and consular missions has been.

I hope that all those who attach great importance to the transatlantic cultural exchange view this Award Ceremony as encouragement.

Sincerely,

Helmut Kohl

Translation: Olaf Unsoeld

1998

Uta Hagen

Piscator Award, American Actress and Acting Teacher, 1919 – 2004
Piscator Preis, Amerikanische Schauspielerin und Schauspiellehrerin, 1919 – 2004

Uta Hagen was born in Germany and came to the United States in 1924 with her parents. She trained briefly at the Royal Academy of Dramatic Arts in London, and then made her Broadway debut in 1938 as Nina in Chekov's *The Sea Gull*. In 1947 she joined the faculty of the Herbert Berghof Studio. She continued to teach there until her death, having trained many of the outstanding actors of the American stage and screen. She and Herbert Berghof were married in 1957.

In 1948 she had phenomenal success as Blanche DuBois in Tennessee Williams' *A Streetcar Named Desire* with Anthony Quinn. In 1962, she originated the role of Martha in Edward Albee's *Who's Afraid of Virginia Woolf?*

Uta Hagen is the author of *Respect for Acting*, which is used as a textbook for many college acting classes, and *A Challenge for the Actor*.

She won the Tony Award three times and was inducted into the American Theater Hall of Fame in 1981.

Uta Hagen wurde in Deutschland geboren und kam 1924 mit ihren Eltern in die USA. Sie absolvierte einen Teil ihrer Ausbildung an der Royal Academy of Dramatic Arts in London und gab 1938 ihr Broadway-Debüt als Nina in Tschechows *Die Möwe*. 1947 wurde sie Schauspiellehrerin am Herbert Berghof Studio. Dort unterrichtete sie bis zu ihrem Tod und bildete viele hervorragende amerikanische Bühnen- und Filmschauspieler aus. 1957 heiratete sie Herbert Berghof.

1948 hatte sie einen sagenhaften Erfolg als Blanche DuBois in Tennessee Williams' *Endstation Sehnsucht* mit Anthony Quinn. 1962 spielte sie die Rolle der Martha in der Uraufführung von *Wer hat Angst vor Virginia Woolf?*

Uta Hagen schrieb *Respect for Acting*, das als Textbuch für den Schauspielunterricht an Colleges verwendet wird, und *A Challenge for the Actor*.

Sie gewann drei Mal den Tony Award und wurde 1981 in die amerikanische Theatre Hall of Fame aufgenommen.

Martha W. Coigney

Honorary Piscator Award, American Director of the International Theatre Institute
Piscator Ehrenpreis, Amerikanische Direktorin des Internationalen Theaterinstituts

For 37 years, from 1966 until 2003, Martha W. Coigney worked for the International Theatre Institute (ITI) of the US and the International Theatre Institute Worldwide. From 1971 until her retirement she was a Member of the Executive Committee of the ITI/Worldwide and from 1987 until 1995 she served as President of ITI/Worldwide.

In 1995, she was awarded UNESCO'S Picasso Medal for service and commitment to international culture and understanding, and was made Honorary President of ITI for life. Founded in 1948 in Prague, the International Theatre Institute started with eight countries and now has a membership of more than 90 countries on five continents. Its mission is the exchange of knowledge and practice in the theatre arts.

Since theater people do not retire, she currently serves on several boards, consults and participates in international theatre projects.

37 Jahre, von 1966 bis 2003, arbeitete Martha W. Coigney beim Internationalen Theaterinstitut (ITI) der USA und dem weltweiten ITI. Von 1971 bis zu ihrem Ausscheiden war sie Mitglied des Exekutivkomitees des weltweiten ITI und von 1987 bis 1995 dessen Präsidentin.

1995 erhielt sie vom ITI den Titel einer Ehrenpräsidentin auf Lebzeit und wurde mit der Picasso Medaille der UNESCO ausgezeichnet. Das Internationale Theaterinstitut, 1948 in Prag gegründet, begann mit acht Ländern und hat nun über 90 Mitgliedsländer auf fünf Kontinenten. Die Zielsetzung des ITI ist der Austausch von Wissen und Praxis in den theatralischen Künsten.

Weil Theaterleute nicht in Ruhestand gehen, ist Martha Coigney derzeit in mehreren Vorständen tätig, berät und wirkt bei internationalen Theaterprojekten mit.

GEORGE E. PATAKI
GOVERNOR

March 19, 1998

Dear Friends:

It is a pleasure to send greetings to all in attendance at the Eleventh Annual Erwin Piscator Award Ceremony.

The Empire State's rich cultural heritage is a source of great pride to all New Yorkers. Institutions that advance the progress and appreciation of the arts merit praise and recognition for their contributions. On this occasion, as Elysium - Between Two Continents shines the light of public tribute upon your esteemed honorees, I am pleased to join in congratulating the renowned actress and teacher, Ms. Uta Hagen, upon receiving the 1998 Erwin Piscator Award; and also the Director of the New York-based International Theatre Institute of the United States, Ms. Martha Coigney, recipient of your honorary award. Your honorees are eminently deserving of the accolades bestowed from an organization such as Elysium - Between Two Continents, which works assiduously to build an intercultural bridge of understanding and exchange between the United States and Europe, especially Germany.

Best wishes to all for a successful evening at the Goethe Institut New York.

Very truly yours,

George E. Pataki

Grußwort des Gouverneurs des Staates New York
George E. Pataki, New York, 19. März 1998

Liebe Freunde,

gerne sende ich Grüße an alle, die zur Elften Jährlichen Erwin Piscator Preisverleihungszeremonie versammelt sind.

Das reiche kulturelle Erbe des Empire State ist für alle New Yorker Grund zu großem Stolz. Institutionen, die die Entwicklung und die Wertschätzung der Künste vorantreiben, verdienen Lob und Wertschätzung für ihre Leistungen. Heute, da Elysium – between two continents Ihre geschätzten Preisträger ins Scheinwerferlicht öffentlicher Anerkennung rückt, ist es mir eine Freude, mit Ihnen gemeinsam die bekannte Schauspielerin und Lehrerin Uta Hagen zu beglückwünschen zu ihrer Auszeichnung mit dem Erwin Piscator Preis 1998. Ebenso gratuliere ich Martha W. Coigney, der Direktorin des in New York ansässigen Internationalen Theaterinstituts der Vereinigten Staaten zum Piscator Ehrenpreis. Ihre Preisträger verdienen es in besonderer Weise, von einer Organisation wie Elysium – between two continents ausgezeichnet zu werden, welche emsig daran arbeitet, eine interkulturelle Brücke der Verständigung und des Austausches zwischen den Vereinigten Staaten und Europa, besonders Deutschland, zu bauen.

Ihnen allen beste Wünsche für einen erfolgreichen Abend im Goethe Institut New York.

Mit freundlichen Grüßen,

George E. Pataki

1 On March 19, 1998, Annegret Decker (left) and Michael Lahr welcome Anne Kaufman Schneider (right) to the Piscator Award at the Goethe Institut. Ms. Kaufman Schneider accepted the award on behalf of Uta Hagen who couldn't make it

2 First row (from left) Christopher Martin, who spoke about Martha Coigney, Rodolphe Coigney, Dr. Cornel Metternich, and Gregorij von Leïtis; Second row (from left): William M. Hoffman, Dr. Norbert Fischer, Kathleen A. Moskal, and Michael Lahr

3 Gregorij von Leïtis applauds Martha W. Coigney, recipient of the Honorary Piscator Award

1 Annegret Decker (links) begrüßt im Beisein von Michael Lahr am 19. März 1998 Anne Kaufman Schneider (rechts) zur Piscator Preisverleihung im Goethe Institut. Frau Kaufman Schneider nahm den Preis in Vertretung für die kurzfristig verhinderte Uta Hagen entgegen.

2 1. Reihe (v.l.n.r.) Christopher Martin, der die Laudatio auf Martha Coigney hielt, Rodolphe Coigney, Dr. Cornel Metternich und Gregorij von Leïtis; 2. Reihe (v.l.n.r.) William M. Hoffman, Dr. Norbert Fischer, Kathleen A. Moskal und Michael Lahr

3 Gregorij von Leïtis applaudiert der Ehrenpreisträgerin Martha W. Coigney

Übersetzung: Michael Lahr

1991

Tony Randall

Piscator Award, American Actor, Director, and Producer, 1920 – 2004
Piscator Preis, Amerikanischer Schauspieler, Regisseur und Produzent, 1920 – 2004

Born in Tulsa, Oklahoma, Tony Randall studied at Columbia University in New York and the Neighborhood Playhouse with Sanford Meisner. He had his theater debut in 1941 in Klabund's *The Chalk Circle*. The Edward Chodorov comedy *Oh, Men! Oh, Women!* really established him in the theater.

He is probably best known for his role as Felix Unger in the television adaptation of Neil Simon's play *The Odd Couple*, opposite Jack Klugman. Among his major film appearances are *Let's Make Love* opposite Marilyn Monroe, *The Mating Game* with Debbie Reynolds, and the trilogy of his Doris Day-Rock Hudson movies, *Pillow Talk*, *Send Me No Flowers*, and *Lover Come Back*.

In 1991, Tony Randall achieved his dream with the launching of his National Actors Theatre, a not-for-profit subscription-based company formed to bring the great classical repertoire of the world, with the finest actors, to a theater that is within reach of all. Until his death in 2004 he was the company's artistic director.

Geboren in Tulsa, Oklahoma, studierte Tony Randall an der Columbia University in New York und am Neighborhood Playhouse mit Sanford Meisner. 1941 hatte er sein Theaterdebüt in Klabunds *Kreidekreis*. Mit Edward Chodorovs Komödie *Oh, Men! Oh, Women!* gelang ihm wirklich der Durchbruch.

Weithin bekannt wurde er durch seine Rolle als Felix Unger in der Fernsehbearbeitung von Neil Simons Stück *Männerwirtschaft* mit Jack Klugman. Zu seinen namhaften Filmauftritten zählen *Machen wir's in Liebe* mit Marilyn Monroe, *Engel unter Sündern* mit Debbie Reynolds, und die Trilogie der Doris Day-Rock Hudson Filme, *Bettgeflüster*, *Schick mir keine Blumen* und *Ein Pyjama für zwei*.

1991 erfüllte sich Tony Randall einen lang gehegten Traum und gründete das National Actors Theatre, eine gemeinnützige Theaterkompanie auf Abonnentenbasis, die das große klassische Repertoire des Welttheaters mit den besten Schauspielern dem breiten Publikum zugänglich machen wollte. Bis zu seinem Tod 2004 war Tony Randall Intendant des National Actors Theatre.

Mary Sharp Cronson

Honorary Piscator Award, American Philanthropist, Founder of Works & Process at the Guggenheim
Piscator Ehrenpreis, Amerikanische Mäzenin, Gründerin von Works & Process at the Guggenheim

For over fifty years, Mary Sharp Cronson has been a member, trustee, or chairperson of numerous cultural boards in New York, including the New York State Council on the Arts, New York City Opera, The Juilliard School and the Solomon R. Guggenheim Foundation.

In 1984, she founded Works & Process at the Guggenheim, a performing arts series designed to showcase creative talent. Choreographers, composers, writers, singers, actors, dancers, costume and set designers, and directors discuss their work and present extended excerpts from current pieces. Thus the audience is treated to a special view which is often inaccessible to the general public. Mary Sharp Cronson continues to be the producer of Works & Process.

In addition, Mary Sharp Cronson was instrumental in bringing the works of young French dance companies to American audiences. And she helped arrange for American artists to become more familiar with French cultural groups.

Seit über 50 Jahren ist Mary Sharp Cronson Vorstandsmitglied oder Vorsitzende zahlreicher kultureller Einrichtungen in New York, darunter New York State Council on the Arts, New York City Opera, Juilliard School und die Solomon R. Guggenheim Foundation.

1984 gründete sie Works & Process at the Guggenheim, eine Serie, in der darstellende Künstler ihr schöpferisches Talent präsentieren. Choreographen, Komponisten, Schriftsteller, Sänger, Schauspieler, Tänzer, Kostüm- und Bühnenbildner und Regisseure diskutieren ihre Arbeit und zeigen Ausschnitte aus kommenden Produktionen. So erhält das Publikum einen seltenen Einblick in den schöpferischen Prozess, quasi hinter die Kulissen. Mary Sharp Cronson ist nach wie vor Produzentin von Works & Process.

Außerdem half Mary Sharp Cronson mit, junge französische Tanzkompanien dem amerikanischen Publikum vorzustellen, und umgekehrt amerikanische Künstler mit französischen Kultureinrichtungen zusammen zu bringen.

1 Among the guests gathered for the 12th Annual Piscator Award on March 15, 1999 at the Goethe Institut were: Heather Randall, Tony Randall, Mary Sharp Cronson, and Gregorij von Leïtis (in the first row from left), and Dr. Stephan Nobbe, Anna Moffo, Dr. Hans-Michael Giesen, and Rick Hobard (in the second row from left)

2 Tony Randall (right) proudly shows the Piscator Award Certificate, which Gregorij von Leïtis has given to him

3 Mary Sharp Cronson, recipient of the Honorary Piscator Award (center), with composer Charles Wuorinen, who spoke about her (right), and Gregorij von Leïtis

1 Zur 12. Piscator Preisverleihung am 15. März 1999 im Goethe Institut versammelten sich: Heather Randall, Tony Randall, Mary Sharp Cronson und Gregorij von Leïtis (in der 1. Reihe v.l.n.r.) und Dr. Stephan Nobbe, Anna Moffo, Dr. Hans-Michael Giesen und Rick Hobard (in der 2. Reihe v.l.n.r.)

2 Tony Randall (rechts) präsentiert stolz die von Gregorij von Leïtis überreichte Piscator Preisurkunde

3 Ehrenpreisträgerin Mary Sharp Cronson (Mitte) mit ihrem Laudator, dem Komponisten Charles Wuorinen (rechts) und Gregorij von Leïtis

» "It was winter, early in '41 – January, February, March," Randall recalls, "and Piscator had a theater down at the New School. I had just graduated from the Neighborhood Playhouse, and I went down and got a part in *The Chalk Circle*, directed by James Light. The ancient Chinese play had been translated into German by Klabund – a great many people at the New School were German refugees."

Piscator, according to Randall, occasionally dropped by the rehearsals, to the consternation of James Light.
"Once or twice Piscator spoke to me," Randall says, "and made some suggestions, which James Light naturally resented. It was a professional company – we were paid $ 15 a week – and Zachary Scott and I made our debuts in this production." Randall, 19 years old at the time, had no idea about Piscator's seminal productions in Germany, nor about his work with Brecht and their creation of Epic Theater. "All his ideas in theater – which I later read about – all that I didn't know about. I was too green to realize that this was an unusual experience."

"I do remember things Piscator said to me. I remember one thing very, very vividly, which had to do with an argument in *The Chalk Circle* about truth versus sophistry: he said, 'Goebbels could not convince Goethe, but Goethe could convince Goebbels.' "

Randall considers the Dramatic Workshop to have been "a wonderful institution," especially for its role in defining modern American acting. «

Excerpts from an article published in Theater Week, December 13, 1993

» "Es war Winter, Anfang 1941 – Januar, Februar, März," erinnert sich Randall, "und Piscator hatte ein Theater unten an der New School. Ich hatte gerade meine Ausbildung am Neighborhood Playhouse beendet, und ich ging dort runter und bekam eine Rolle im *Kreidekreis*, den James Light inszenierte. Das alte chinesische Stück war von Klabund ins Deutsche übertragen worden – ein großer Teil der Leute an der New School waren deutsche Flüchtlinge."

Piscator, so Randall, kam gelegentlich zu den Proben, zur Bestürzung von James Light. „Einmal oder zweimal sprach Piscator mit mir," sagt Randall, „er machte Vorschläge, die James Light natürlich verägerten. Es war ein professionelles Theater – wir bekamen $ 15 die Woche – und Zachary Scott und ich hatten mit diesem Stück unser Theaterdebüt." Randall, damals 19 Jahre alt, hatte keine Ahnung von Piscators bahnbrechenden Inszenierungen in Deutschland, wusste auch nichts von dessen Arbeit mit Brecht und der Gründung des Epischen Theaters. „All seine Ideen über das Theater, von denen ich später las, waren mir damals unbekannt. Ich war zu naiv, um zu erkennen, dass dies eine außergewöhnliche Erfahrung war."

„Ich erinnere mich an Dinge, die Piscator zu mir sagte. Eine Sache ist mir besonders lebhaft in Erinnerung; sie hatte zu tun mit einer Auseinandersetzung im *Kreidekreis* über Wahrheit im Vergleich zu Sophisterei. Er sagte: ‚Goebbels hätte Goethe nicht überzeugen können, aber Goethe konnte Goebbels überzeugen'."

Randall hält den Dramatic Workshop für eine „wunderbare Einrichtung", besonders hinsichtlich der prägenden Rolle, die er für das moderne amerikanische Schauspiel hatte. «

Auszug aus einem Artikel, veröffentlicht in Theater Week, 13. Dezember 1993

2000

Ellen Burstyn

Piscator Award, American Actress, born 1932
Piscator Preis, Amerikanische Schauspielerin, geboren 1932

Ellen Burstyn's illustrious career encompasses stage, film, and television. She debuted on Broadway in 1957 in *Fair Game*. Her starring role in *Same Time, Next Year* in 1975 brought her a Tony Award as Best Actress. Other theatre credits include the 1982 Broadway production of *84 Charing Cross Road*, the one-woman play *Shirley Valentine*, *Shimada*, and *Sacrilege*. She also starred in Eugene O'Neill's *Long Day's Journey into Night*.

Her portrait of an ex-housewife turned waitress and singer trying to support herself and her 12-year-old-son, in *Alice Doesn't Live Here Anymore* won her the Oscar for Best Actress in 1974. She has been nominated for Oscars as best actress in three other film roles, *The Exorcist*, *Resurrection*, and *Requiem for a Dream*.

In the 1970s, Burstyn was active in the movement to free convicted boxer Rubin "Hurricane" Carter from jail. Burstyn was the first woman to be elected President of Actors' Equity Association and served as the Artistic Director of the Actors Studio for six years, where she studied with the late Lee Strasberg.

Ellen Burstyns glänzende Karriere umfaßt Bühne, Film und Fernsehen. 1957 debütierte sie am Broadway in *Fair Game*. Ihre Hauptrolle in *Nächstes Jahr, selbe Zeit* brachte ihr 1975 den Tony Award als beste Schauspielerin. Andere Theatererfolge waren *84 Charing Cross Road* (1982 am Broadway), das Ein-Personen-Stück *Shirley Valentine*, *Shimada* und *Sacrilege*. Sie spielte auch die Hauptrolle in Eugene O'Neills *Eines langen Tages Reise in die Nacht*.

Für ihre Darstellung einer Hausfrau, die zur Kellnerin und Sängerin wird, um sich und ihren 12jährigen Sohn durchzubringen im Film *Alice lebt hier nicht mehr* gewann sie 1974 den Oscar als beste Schauspielerin. Sie wurde für drei weitere Filme für den Oscar nominiert: *Der Exorzist*, *Der starke Wille* und *Requiem for a Dream*.

In den 70er Jahren engagierte sie sich für die Freilassung des verurteilten Boxers Rubin „Hurricane" Carter aus dem Gefängnis. Burstyn war die erste gewählte Präsidentin der Gewerkschaft Actors' Equity und sechs Jahre lang Leiterin des Actors Studios, wo sie bei Lee Strasberg studiert hatte.

Anna-Maria Kellen

Honorary Piscator Award, American Philanthropist
Piscator Ehrenpreis, Amerikanische Mäzenin

Born in Berlin, Germany, Anna-Maria Kellen served on the board of directors of the Third Street Music School Settlement New York for many years. In addition she was a board member of the Parsons School of Design, the Cancer Research Institute in New York City, the Metropolitan Museum of Art, among numerous other institutions. For ten years she served as a member of the Commission for Cultural Affairs of the City of New York.

Die gebürtige Berlinerin Anna-Maria Kellen engagierte sich viele Jahre lang im Vorstand des Third Street Music School Settlement New York. Außerdem war sie u.a. in den Vorständen der Parsons School of Design, des Krebsforschungsinstituts New York und des Metropolitan Museums. Zehn Jahre lang war sie ehrenamtliches Mitglied des Kulturdezernates der Stadt New York.

Stephen M. Kellen

Honorary Piscator Award, American Banker and Philanthropist, 1914 – 2004
Piscator Ehrenpreis, Amerikanischer Bankier und Mäzen, 1914 – 2004

Stephen M. Kellen was Co-Chairman of Arnhold & S. Bleichroeder Holdings, Inc. In his native Berlin, he helped realize The American Academy in Berlin, which was established in the former childhood home of Mrs. Kellen, née Arnhold. He also served on many boards, among others as a trustee at Carnegie Hall Society, the National Gallery of Art in Washington, D.C. and WNET/ Channel Thirteen. Numerous institutions have benefitted from Anna-Maria and Stephen M. Kellen's tireless efforts.

Stephen M. Kellen war Co-Chairman von Arnhold & S. Bleichroeder Holdings, Inc. In seiner Geburtsstadt Berlin half er, im Elternhaus seiner Frau die American Academy in Berlin zu etablieren. Er engagierte sich in den Vorständen vieler Kultureinrichtungen, u.a. als Trustee der Carnegie Hall Society, der National Gallery of Art in Washington, D.C. und des gemeinnützigen Senders WNET / Channel Thirteen. Zahlreichen Organisationen kam der unermüdliche Einsatz des Ehepaares Kellen zugute.

1 As a surprise guest, violinist Isaac Stern thanks Mr. and Mrs. Kellen for their support of Carnegie Hall

2 Dr. Christoph Thun-Hohenstein, Kathleen A. Moskal, who chaired the Piscator Luncheon Committee, New York's Cultural Commissioner Schuyler G. Chapin, Jody Arnhold, and Director Arthur Penn (*Bonnie & Clyde*) (from left)

3 The Austrian Consul General Dr. Harald Miltner, Almut Giesen, and Carroll Brown, President of the American Council on Germany (from left)

4 Ellen Burstyn

5 Michael M. Kellen, Edna Lind, Michael Lahr, and Denise Kellen at the 13th Piscator Award Luncheon on April 11, 2000 at the Hotel Plâza Athénée (from left)

6 Gregorij von Leïtis (left) presents Anna-Maria and Stephen M. Kellen with the Honorary Piscator Award, after Kurt F. Viermetz (2nd from right) had spoken in their honor

1 Violinist Isaac Stern dankte als Überraschungsgast dem Ehepaar Kellen für seine Unterstützung der Carnegie Hall

2 Dr. Christoph Thun-Hohenstein, Kathleen A. Moskal, die den Vorsitz des Piscator Luncheon Komitees hatte, New Yorks Kulturdezernent Schuyler G. Chapin, Jody Arnhold und US-Regisseur Arthur Penn (*Bonnie & Clyde*) (v.l.n.r.)

3 Österreichs Generalkonsul Dr. Harald Miltner, Almut Giesen und Carroll Brown, Präsident des American Council on Germany (v.l.n.r.)

4 Ellen Burstyn

5 Michael M. Kellen, Edna Lind, Michael Lahr und Denise Kellen beim 13. Piscator Preis am 11. April 2000 im Hotel Plâza Athénée (v.l.n.r.)

6 Gregorij von Leïtis (links) überreicht Anna-Maria und Stephen M. Kellen den Piscator Ehrenpreis, nachdem Kurt F. Viermetz (2.v.r.) die Laudatio gehalten hatte

» I met Ellen Burstyn hard at work at the Actors Studio in 1981 at a time in her life when she could have rightly sat back on her laurels. By then, she had already been nominated for several Academy Awards. […] But here she was, a true star, an artist devoted to her craft […] What I saw was a fellow actor who supported the entire environment there, artistic and human. I recall her once saying to a young actor: "Don't beat yourself up here. There is no wrong. There's just another way to try it and strive for development."[…]

Why the Piscator Award? Erwin Piscator's emphasis was not merely on presenting a political theater but on the theater as a continuing exploration of the individual's ability to affect change in society and the universe. So see our honoree in the movie *Hurricane* and in it you will see her in some historical footage as the real-life Ellen Burstyn with Bob Dylan and others standing up for Rubin Hurricane Carter, the disenfranchised and human rights. As an actress, in her many characters, she teaches us about social awareness, human behavior, and human logic. She all-inclusively embraces the world and strives for understanding, love and support in her work and as a person.
Or should she receive this award for continuing a certain lineage of the theater? Piscator taught Lee Strasberg and Ellen Burstyn studied with Lee Strasberg. She continues to mold the theater of tomorrow […]

In the movie *Resurrection*, Ellen Burstyn portrayed a faith healer. Many people today have lost faith in the power of theater and think it dead. In her life and work, Ellen Burstyn has healed and resurrected faith in the theater for multitudes of actors and theater goers. «

Gregorij von Leïtis
Excerpts from his remarks on Ellen Burstyn

» Ich traf Ellen Burstyn erstmals 1981 hart arbeitend im Actors Studio; damals hätte sie sich schon zu Recht auf ihren Lorbeeren ausruhen können; sie war bereits mehrmals für den Oscar nominiert worden. […] Aber hier war sie, ein wirklicher Star, eine Künstlerin, ganz ihrer Zunft hingegeben […] Ich erlebte eine Schauspielkollegin, die ihr ganzes Umfeld unterstützte, künstlerisch und menschlich. Einem jungen Schauspieler sagte sie einmal: „Machen Sie sich nicht fertig. Was Sie tun, ist nicht falsch. Es gibt nur verschiedene Arten des Probierens und der Entwicklung." […]

Warum der Piscator Preis? Erwin Piscators Augenmerk lag nicht nur auf dem politischen Theater sondern auf einem Theater, das permanent die Möglichkeiten des Einzelnen erkundete, Wandel in der Gesellschaft und in der Welt zu bewirken.
Schauen wir uns unsere Preisträgerin in dem Film *Hurricane* an. Darin sehen wir die echte Ellen Burstyn in historischen Aufnahmen, wie sie mit Bob Dylan und anderen eintritt für Rubin Hurricane Carter, die Entrechteten und die Menschenrechte. Als Schauspielerin führt sie uns in ihren diversen Rollen soziales Bewusstsein, menschliches Verhalten und menschliche Logik vor Augen. Integrierend umspannt sie die Welt und bemüht sich in ihrer Arbeit und als Person um Verständigung, Zuwendung und Unterstützung.
Oder sollte sie diesen Preis bekommen, weil sie eine gewisse Traditionslinie des Theaters fortsetzt? Piscator unterrichtete Lee Strasberg, und Ellen Burstyn studierte bei Lee Strasberg. Sie prägt das Theater von morgen. […]

Im Film *Resurrection* stellt Ellen Burstyn einen Gesundbeter dar. Viele Menschen heute haben den Glauben an die Macht des Theaters verloren und halten es für tot. Durch ihr Leben und ihre Arbeit hat Ellen Burstyn den Glauben an das Theater geheilt und auferweckt für eine Vielzahl von Schauspielern und Theaterbesuchern. «

Gregorij von Leïtis
Auszug aus seiner Laudatio auf Ellen Burstyn

THE WHITE HOUSE

WASHINGTON

April 10, 2000

Warm greetings to all those gathered for the presentation of the 13th annual Erwin Piscator Award by Elysium -- Between Two Continents. I am delighted to join you in congratulating this year's award recipients, Ellen Burstyn and Anna-Maria and Stephen Kellen.

In their many forms, the arts add immeasurably to the quality of our lives. They open our eyes, ears, and imagination; they challenge our assumptions; they can even change the way we see ourselves and the world. Giving voice to our dreams and opening doors to other experiences and cultures, the arts can take us beyond our everyday lives and provide unforgettable moments of joy and insight.

This year's honorees have contributed much to this important legacy through their talents, vision, and generous spirit. I am proud to salute them for their many accomplishments, and I send best wishes to all for a memorable event.

Grußwort des Präsidenten der Vereinigten Staaten von Amerika
Bill Clinton, Washington, 10. April 2000

Freundliche Grüße an alle, die zur Verleihung des 13. Jährlichen Erwin
Piscator Preises durch Elysium – between two continents versammelt sind.
Es freut mich sehr, zusammen mit Ihnen den diesjährigen Preisträgern, Ellen
Burstyn und Anna-Maria und Stephen Kellen, zu gratulieren.

In ihren vielen Formen tragen die Künste unschätzbar bei zur Qualität
unseres Lebens. Sie öffnen unsere Augen, Ohren und Vorstellungskraft; sie
fordern unsere Anschauungen heraus; sie können sogar die Art und Weise
ändern, wie wir uns selbst und die Welt sehen. Indem sie unseren Träumen
eine Stimme geben und Türen öffnen zu anderen Erfahrungen und Kulturen,
können die Künste uns über unser tägliches Leben hinaus führen und uns
unvergessliche Momente der Freude und der Einsicht gewähren.

Die diesjährigen Preisträger haben Großes beigetragen zu diesem
wichtigen Erbe durch ihre Talente, ihre Vision und ihren großzügigen Geist.
Ich bin stolz, ihnen für ihre vielfältigen Leistungen meine Anerkennung
zum Ausdruck zu bringen, und sende allen beste Wünsche für einen
unvergesslichen Festakt.

Bill Clinton

Übersetzung: Michael Lahr

2001

Anne Jackson

Piscator Award, American Actress, born 1926
Piscator Preis, Amerikanische Schauspielerin, geboren 1926

Trained at the Neighborhood Playhouse and the Actors Studio, Jackson made her debut in Chekov's *The Cherry Orchard*. She and her husband of 64 years, actor Eli Wallach, have frequently acted together. Her screen appearances include *Golda* with Ingrid Bergman, Stanley Kubrick's *The Shining*, *The Secret Life of an American Wife* with Walter Matthau, and *Dirty Dingus McGhee* with Frank Sinatra.

Nach dem Schauspieltraining im Neighborhood Playhouse und im Actors Studio, debütierte Jackson in Tschechows *Der Kirschgarten*. 1948 heiratete sie den Schauspieler Eli Wallach, mit dem sie seither vielfach zusammen spielte. Zu ihren wichtigen Filmen zählen *Golda* mit Ingrid Bergman, Stanley Kubricks *Shining*, *The Secret Life of an American Wife* mit Walter Matthau und *Dirty Dingus, der scharfe Bandit* mit Frank Sinatra.

Eli Wallach

Piscator Award, American Actor, born 1915
Piscator Preis, Amerikanischer Schauspieler, geboren 1915

Eli Wallach attended the Actors Studio and met his wife, Anne Jackson, in his stage debut, an Off-Broadway production of Tennessee Williams' *This Property is Condemned*. A leading interpreter of Williams' work, he appeared in *The Rose Tattoo* and *Camino Real*. After his film debut in Elia Kazan's *Baby Doll*, Wallach had a prolific career. His film credits include: *The Magnificent Seven*, *The Good, the bad, and the Ugly*, *The Godfather III*, and as recently as 2010, *Wall Street: Money Never Sleeps*, and *The Ghost Writer*.

Eli Wallach studierte am Actors Studio und traf seine Frau Anne Jackson bei seinem Bühnendebüt, in der Off-Broadway-Produktion von Tennessee Williams *Dieses Mädchen ist für alle*. Als führender Interpret von Williams Stücken spielte Wallach auch in *Die tätowierte Rose* und *Camino Real* mit. Nach seinem Filmdebüt in Elia Kazans *Baby Doll*, hatte Wallach eine produktive Karriere: Er wirkte mit bei *Die glorreichen Sieben*, *Zwei glorreiche Halunken*, *Der Pate III*, und – erst im Jahre 2010 – in *Wall Street: Geld schläft nicht* und *Der Ghostwriter*.

Dr. Ellen Hedda Landesmann

Honorary Piscator Award, Austrian Philanthropist, born 1935
Piscator Ehrenpreis, Österreichische Mäzenin, geboren 1935

For more than five decades, Ellen Landesmann has been active in a number of organizations, such as the Society of the Friends of Fine Arts, and the International Committee for Voluntary Social Help in Austria. Since 1989 she has been president of the Austrian Society of the Friends of the Hebrew University in Jerusalem and helped arrange a partnership agreement for scientific exchange between the University of Vienna and the Hebrew University of Jerusalem.

Seit über fünf Jahrzehnten ist Ellen Landesmann aktiv in einer Reihe von Organisationen, darunter die Gesellschaft der Freunde der Bildenden Künste und das Internationale Komitee für freiwillige Sozialhilfe Österreichs. Seit 1989 ist sie Präsidentin der Österreichischen Gesellschaft der Freunde der Hebräischen Universität Jerusalem und half mit, ein Abkommen zum wissenschaftlichen Austausch zwischen der Uni Wien und der Hebräischen Universität zu vermitteln.

Dr. Peter Landesmann

Honorary Piscator Award, Austrian Philanthropist, born 1929
Piscator Ehrenpreis, Österreichischer Mäzen, geboren 1929

In Peter Landesmann's philanthropic activities the Christian-Jewish dialogue plays a very important role; he is a board member of the Christian-Jewish Coordination Committee. The author of several books (The Jews and their Faith, and Rabbis from Vienna), Landesmann also is active on the board of the Friends of the Vienna State Opera, and was president of the Friends of the Vienna Museum of Art Nouveau and the Association for the Support of Austrian Contemporary Music.

Der christlich-jüdische Dialog spielt für Peter Landesmann eine besonders wichtige Rolle; er ist Vorstandsmitglied des Christlich-Jüdischen Koordinierungs-Ausschusses. Als Autor diverser Bücher (u.a. Die Juden und ihr Glaube und Rabbiner aus Wien) ist Landesmann auch aktiv im Vorstand der Freunde der Wiener Staatsoper und war Präsident der Freunde des Wiener Jugendstilmuseums und des Vereins zur Förderung österreichischer Gegenwartsmusik.

Der Bundespräsident

It is my pleasure to send greetings to all present at the 2001 Erwin Piscator Award Ceremony. Four outstanding personalities are to be honored whose contributions to the theatre and to the arts are truly commendable.

Anne Jackson and Eli Wallach have consistently devoted their distinguished careers to serious drama. Through their many successful appearances on stage as well as in films and on television they touch the lives of captivated audiences worldwide. I am very pleased to join you in recognizing these two great artists.

Peter and Ellen Landesmann from Vienna have excelled over the years in closely associating their lives with the arts by supporting them in a singularly dedicated manner. They are wonderful role models and second to none in their unfailing and exemplary commitment to the arts. I am delighted that they receive this well-deserved recognition and I take great pleasure in extending my congratulations.

We should all be grateful for the profound dedication of the honorees, which is nourished by the arts and which sustains the arts to the benefit of society at large.

I send my best wishes and gladly join Elysium Between Two Continents in honoring the recipients of this prestigious award whose name now rightly includes the memory of Maria Ley Piscator, a native of Vienna, who had enriched the genius of her husband with her cultural heritage.

Grußwort des Bundespräsidenten der Republik Österreich
Thomas Klestil, 2001

Gerne sende ich Grüße an alle, die zur Erwin Piscator Preisverleihung 2001 versammelt sind. Vier herausragende Persönlichkeiten werden geehrt, deren Leistungen auf dem Gebiet des Theaters und der Künste wirklich vorbildlich sind.

Anne Jackson und Eli Wallach haben ihre distinguierten Karrieren beständig in den Dienst des ernsthaften Theaters gestellt. Durch ihre vielen erfolgreichen Auftritte auf der Bühne, in Filmen und im Fernsehen haben sie die Existenzen faszinierter Zuschauer weltweit berührt. Es freut mich außerordentlich, mit Ihnen diesen beiden großen Künstlern meine Anerkennung auszusprechen.

Peter und Ellen Landesmann aus Wien haben sich über die Jahre hervorgetan durch ihre einzigartige hingebungsvolle Förderung der Künste. Sie sind wunderbare Vorbilder und unübertroffen in ihrem unerschöpflichen und beispielhaften Engagement für die Künste. Ich bin erfreut, dass sie diese wohlverdiente Auszeichnung erhalten und gratuliere sehr herzlich.

Wir sollten alle dankbar sein für den tiefgreifenden Einsatz der Geehrten, der sich speist aus den Künsten und der die Künste stärkt zum Wohl der Gesellschaft als Ganzer.

Ich sende meine besten Wünsche und freue mich, mit Elysium – between two continents die Gewinner dieses prestigeträchtigen Preises zu ehren, dessen Name nun zu Recht auch das Andenken an Maria Ley Piscator umfasst, einer gebürtigen Wienerin, die das Genie ihres Mannes bereicherte durch ihr kulturelles Erbe.

Thomas Klestil

Übersetzung: Michael Lahr

1 Rabbi Arthur Schneier (left), president of the Appeal of Conscience Foundation, and his wife Elisabeth, sign the guest book of the Piscator Award Luncheon on March 22, 2001 at the Lotos Club in New York

2 Anne Jackson (right) and Eli Wallach (center) thank Gregorij von Leïtis and the guests for the 14th Erwin Piscator Award

3 Ellen Hedda Landesmann (right) and her husband Peter (left) happily accept the Honorary Piscator Award 2001 from Gregorij von Leïtis

1 Rabbi Arthur Schneier (links), Präsident der Appeal of Conscience Foundation, und seine Frau Elisabeth tragen sich am 22. März 2001 im New Yorker Lotos Club ins Gästebuch ein

2 Anne Jackson (rechts) und Eli Wallach (Mitte) danken Gregorij von Leïtis und den Gästen für die Auszeichnung mit dem 14. Erwin Piscator Preis

3 Ellen Hedda Landesmann (rechts) und ihr Mann Peter (links) freuen sich über den von Gregorij von Leïtis überreichten Piscator Ehrenpreis 2001

Kurt Masur

Piscator Award, German Conductor and Humanist, born 1927
Piscator Preis, Deutscher Dirigent und Humanist, geboren 1927

Kurt Masur is one of the most widely respected musicians of his generation and a frequent guest conductor with the world's leading orchestras. For many seasons, Maestro Masur served as Gewandhaus Kapellmeister of the Leipzig Gewandhaus; in this capacity he led nearly 1000 performances between 1970 and 1996 and more than 900 concerts on tour.

In 1989, he played a central role during the peaceful demonstrations in Leipzig that led to the German reunification.

From 1991 until 2002 he was Music Director of the New York Philharmonic, and in 2002 he was appointed Music Director of the Orchestre National de France in Paris. Kurt Masur has made well over 100 recordings, including the complete symphonies of Beethoven, Brahms, Bruckner, Mendelssohn, Schumann, and Tchaikovsky. In 2008 he celebrated 60 years as a professional conductor.

Education is very important to Maestro Masur. He often conducts youth orchestras and gives master classes.

Kurt Masur ist einer der meist-respektierten Musiker seiner Generation und regelmäßig zu Gast bei den führenden Orchestern der Welt. Viele Jahre lang war er Kapellmeister des Gewandhauses in Leipzig und dirigierte von 1970 bis 1996 fast 1000 Aufführungen und mehr als 900 Konzerte auf den verschiedenen Tourneen dieses Orchesters.

1989 spielte er eine zentrale Rolle während der friedlichen Montagsdemonstrationen in Leipzig, die zur deutschen Wiedervereinigung führten.

Von 1991 bis 2002 war er Musikdirektor des New York Philharmonic Orchestra; 2002 wurde er Musikdirektor des Orchestre National de France in Paris. Kurt Masur hat weit über 100 Platten und CDs eingespielt, u.a. die kompletten Symphonien von Beethoven, Brahms, Bruckner, Mendelssohn, Schumann und Tschaikowsky. 2008 feierte er sein 60jähriges Jubiläum als Dirigent.

Erziehung spielt für Maestro Masur eine große Rolle. Deshalb leitet er oft Jugendorchester und gibt Meisterklassen.

Dr. Bernd-A. von Maltzan

Honorary Piscator Award, German Banker and Philanthropist, born 1949
Piscator Ehrenpreis, Deutscher Banker und Mäzen, geboren 1949

Until his retirement in 2011, Dr. Bernd-A. von Maltzan was the Vice Chairman of Deutsche Bank's global division Private Wealth Management. Before that, he was responsible for the build-up of the Private Banking division. Until 1996 he headed Deutsche Bank's investment banking in Germany. Prior to that, Dr. von Maltzan was global head of Trading & Sales at Deutsche Bank. Dr. von Maltzan is a member of several advisory boards in privately held companies.

Dr. von Maltzan has been devoting his energy, time and work to the support of the arts and education. Among others, he has been Chairman of the Königswinter Foundation (German-British Society) and is the Founding President of the American Berlin Opera Foundation, New York. He has been an avid supporter of the Heidelberg Center for American Studies, and an advisor for the Organisation SOS Childrens' Villages. He also founded a circle of friends which since 1988 has been working to bring together families from the eastern and western part of Germany.

Bis zu seiner Pensionierung 2011 war Dr. Bernd-A. von Maltzan Bereichsvorstand der Deutschen Bank für das globale Private Wealth Management. Ab 1996 baute er das weltweite Private Banking Geschäft auf. Bis dahin war er Leiter des Investmentbankings Deutschland und zuvor Direktor mit Generalvollmacht für Trading & Sales. Dr. von Maltzan hat diverse Aufsichtsratsmandate.

Dr. von Maltzan widmet seine Energie, Zeit und Arbeit der Unterstützung von Kunst und Bildung. Er ist in verschiedenen gemeinnützigen Organisationen aktiv, unter anderem als Vorsitzender des Kuratoriums der Königswinter Stiftung (eine deutsch-englische Gesellschaft) und als Gründungspräsident der American Berlin Opera Foundation, New York, einem amerikanischen Förderkreis der Deutschen Oper in Berlin. Er fördert das Heidelberg Center for American Studies und ist im Beirat der SOS Kinderdörfer. Auf seine Initiative hin wurde 1988 ein Freundeskreis zur Begegnung ostdeutscher und westdeutscher Familien gegründet.

1 Andrea Countess Bernstorff, the Berlin-based lawyer and art patron Prof. Dr. Peter Raue, Eva Wagner-Pasquier, who has been serving as Co-Artistic Director of the Bayreuth Festival since 2008, and Gregorij von Leïtis (from left)

2 Dr. Bernd-A. von Maltzan (left) and his wife Ursula (right) with Anna Moffo in the library of the Lotos Club

3 Tomoko Masur (left) and Maestro Kurt Masur (center) arrive at the Lotos Club on April 2, 2002 accompanied by Stefana Atlas

4 The German Consul General in New York Bernhard von der Planitz (standing) reads a message of greeting sent by German Federal President Johannes Rau

1 Andrea Gräfin von Bernstorff, der Berliner Anwalt und Kunstförderer Prof. Dr. Peter Raue, Eva Wagner-Pasquier, die seit 2008 gemeinsam mit ihrer Halbschwester Katharina Wagner die künstlerische Leitung der Bayreuther Festspiele inne hat, und Gregorij von Leïtis (v.l.n.r.)

2 Dr. Bernd-A. von Maltzan (links) und seine Frau Ursula (rechts) mit Anna Moffo in der Bibliothek des Lotos Clubs

3 Tomoko Masur (links) und Maestro Kurt Masur (Mitte) treffen in Begleitung von Stefana Atlas am 2. April 2002 zur Piscator Preisverleihung im Lotos Club ein

4 Der deutsche Generalkonsul in New York Bernhard von der Planitz (stehend) verliest die Grußbotschaft von Bundespräsident Johannes Rau

5 The two sopranos Beverly Sills (left) and Anna Moffo (right) with Super-Model Carmen Dell'Orefice

6 Dr. Herbert Cohen and Rhoda Weiskopf Cohen

7 Carmen Dell'Orefice (left), Dr. Hans Peter Mauch (center), and Margaret J. Leytess-Hoffman

8 Beverly Sills praises the enormous achievements of Kurt Masur

9 Speaker Kurt F. Viermetz (right) congratulates honoree Dr. Bernd-A. von Maltzan (left), while Gregorij von Leïtis is looking on

5 Die beiden Soprane Beverly Sills (links) und Anna Moffo (rechts) mit Super-Model Carmen Dell'Orefice

6 Das Ehepaar Dr. Herbert Cohen und Rhoda Weiskopf Cohen

7 Carmen Dell'Orefice (links), Dr. Hans Peter Mauch (Mitte) und Margaret J. Leytess-Hoffman

8 Beverly Sills würdigt in ihrer Laudatio die Verdienste von Kurt Masur

9 Laudator Kurt F. Viermetz (rechts) gratuliert Ehrenpreisträger Dr. Bernd-A. von Maltzan (links), während Gregorij von Leïtis zuschaut

Berlin, den 25. März 2002

Sehr geehrter Herr von Leïtis,

ich möchte Sie bitten, Herrn Kurt Masur zur Verleihung des Erwin Piscator Awards und Herrn Dr. Bernd-A. von Maltzan zur Verleihung des Erwin Piscator Honorary Awards meine herzlichen Glückwünsche zu übermitteln.

Mit der Preisverleihung an Kurt Masur und Dr. Bernd-A. von Maltzan haben Sie eine gute Wahl getroffen. Das künstlerische Lebenswerk Masurs und das langjährige kulturelle Engagement von Dr. von Maltzan führt uns deutlich vor Augen: Musik und Kunst sind solide Pfeiler der Brücke, die den Atlantik überspannt und die Vereinigten Staaten von Amerika mit Deutschland und Europa verbindet. Musik und Kunst können zum Dialog der Menschen untereinander, zur Verständigung und damit zur Verbesserung der internationalen Beziehungen beitragen.

Das ist heute im Zeitalter der Globalisierung so aktuell wie eh und je. In einer Zeit, in der sich viele Menschen von der Geschwindigkeit, mit der sich unsere Welt verändert, bedroht fühlen, brauchen wir Kunst und Musik, in der sich die Menschen wiederfinden, ganz besonders.

Ich freue mich daher sehr, dass sich Elysium das Bauen von Brücken zwischen den beiden Kontinenten mit den Mitteln der Kunst zur Aufgabe gemacht hat.

In diesem Sinne grüße ich die Teilnehmer Ihres Festaktes.

Mit freundlichen Grüßen

Ihr

Message of the President of the Federal Republic of Germany
Johannes Rau, Berlin, March 25, 2002

Dear Mr. von Leïtis,

I want to ask you, to convey my heartfelt congratulations to Mr. Kurt Masur on the bestowal of the Erwin Piscator Award and to Dr. Bernd-A. von Maltzan on the bestowal of the Erwin Piscator Honorary Award.

With the award being given to Kurt Masur and Dr. Bernd-A. von Maltzan you have made a very good choice. Masur's artistic life achievement and Dr. von Maltzan's longstanding cultural commitment clearly demonstrates: Music and Art are solid piers of the bridge, which spans the Atlantic and connects the United States of America with Germany and Europe. Music and Art can contribute to the dialogue among people, to understanding and thus to the improvement of international relationships. Today, in an age of globalization, this is more urgent than ever. In a time, when many people feel threatened by the pace, with which our world changes, we especially need art and music, in which we find ourselves again.

Therefore, I am very glad, that Elysium has made it its task to build bridges between the two continents by means of art.

In this sense I extend greetings to the participants of your ceremony.

With kind regards,

Yours Johannes Rau

Translation: Paul Tiffan

2003

Anna Moffo

Piscator Award, American Soprano, 1932 – 2006
Piscator Preis, Amerikanische Sopranistin, 1932 – 2006

Although mostly interested in sports during her high school days, Anna Moffo won a scholarship to the Curtis Institute of Music and later studied in Italy. Her very first audition landed her the title role of Cio-Cio San in *Madama Butterfly* in Milan. The performance was televised live and Anna, known ever since as "La Moffo", was an overnight sensation. She was sought after by every opera house and performed with all big orchestras worldwide. Her Metropolitan Opera debut took place in 1959 as Violetta in *La Traviata*, a part that would become her signature role. She performed at the Met for seventeen seasons. Throughout her career she sang 146 major roles.

For twelve years Anna Moffo had her own TV show in Rome. She made numerous recordings, appeared in film versions of *La Traviata* and *Lucia di Lammermoor* and did twelve non-singing films.

After retiring from singing she was active as a board member of the Metropolitan Opera Guild and gave a number of master classes.

Obwohl sie sich hauptsächlich für Sport interessierte, studierte Anna Moffo mit einem Stipendium am Curtis Institute of Music und später in Italien Gesang. Ihr erstes Vorsingen bescherte ihr sogleich die Titelrolle der Cio-Cio San in *Madama Butterfly* in Mailand. Die Vorstellung wurde live im Fernsehen übertragen, und Anna – seitdem bekannt als „La Moffo" – wurde über Nacht zur Sensation. Sie wurde von allen Opernhäusern der Welt begehrt und gastierte mit allen bedeutenden Orchestern. 1959 gab sie ihr Debüt an der Metropolitan Opera als Violetta in *La Traviata*, eine Rolle, die schnell ihr Markenzeichen wurde. 17 Spielzeiten lang stand sie auf der Bühne der Met. Während ihrer gesamten Laufbahn sang sie 146 große Partien.

Zwölf Jahre lang hatte Anna Moffo ihre eigene Fernsehsendung in Rom. Sie spielte zahlreiche Platten und CDs ein, stand in Verfilmungen von *La Traviata* und *Lucia di Lammermoor* vor der Kamera und drehte zwölf weitere Filme.

Nach dem Ende ihrer Gesangskarriere war sie an der Metropolitan Opera Guild aktiv und gab etliche Meisterklassen.

Kurt F. Viermetz

Honorary Piscator Award, German Banker and Philanthropist, born 1939
Piscator Ehrenpreis, Deutscher Banker und Mäzen, geboren 1939

Kurt F. Viermetz has held prominent positions in the international banking community: From 1990 until 1998, he was Vice Chairman of JP Morgan, from 1999 until 2008 he served as Chairman of the Supervisory Board of Bayerische Hypo- und Vereinsbank, and from 2005 until 2008 he was Chairman of the Supervisory Board of Deutsche Börse.

Viermetz is an Honorary Citizen of his hometown Augsburg. He has generously supported the museums, the library and the university in Augsburg. In 2003, he and his late wife Felicitas instituted the Kurt and Felicitas Viermetz Foundation to foster art, culture and science in the Swabian part of Bavaria.

In addition, Kurt Viermetz is a member of the advisory board of the Council on Public Policy, and a trustee of the American Academy in Berlin. He was a board member of the American Council on Germany, and in 2002 was elected honorary director of the New York Philharmonic Society, after having served on its board for 15 years.

Kurt F. Viermetz bekleidete führende Positionen im internationalen Bankenwesen. Von 1990 bis 1998 war er Stellvertretender Vorstandsvorsitzender von JP Morgan, von 1999 bis 2008 war er Aufsichtsratsvorsitzender der Bayerischen Hypo- und Vereinsbank, und von 2005 bis 2008 Chef des Aufsichtsrats der Deutschen Börse AG.

Viermetz ist Ehrenbürger seiner Geburtsstadt Augsburg. Die Museen, die Stadtbücherei und die Universität von Augsburg wurden großzügig von ihm gefördert. 2003 rief er mit seiner verstorbenen Frau Felicitas die Kurt und Felicitas Viermetz Stiftung ins Leben, um Wissenschaft, Kunst und Kultur in Bayerisch-Schwaben zu fördern.

Kurt Viermetz ist darüber hinaus Mitglied des Kuratoriums des Council on Public Policy und Trustee der American Academy in Berlin. Er war im Vorstand des American Council on Germany und wurde 2002 nach 15jähriger ehrenamtlicher Vorstandstätigkeit zum Ehrenmitglied der New Yorker Philharmoniker ernannt.

1 Anna Moffo (right) greets Felicitas Viermetz (left) and her husband Kurt F. Viermetz

2 Gisela and Bernhard von der Planitz in conversation with Peter Sötje and Anna Moffo (from left)

3 Journalist Manuela Hoelterhoff, Rosita Sarnoff, and Tony Randall during the reception prior to the 16th Annual Piscator Award Luncheon on April 2, 2003 at the Lotos Club (from left)

4 Soprano Licia Albanese, Dr. Robert J. Campbell, and Edna Lind (from right)

1 Anna Moffo (rechts) begrüßt Felicitas Viermetz (links) und ihren Mann Kurt F. Viermetz

2 Gisela und Bernhard von der Planitz im Gespräch mit Peter Sötje und Anna Moffo (v.l.n.r.)

3 Journalistin Manuela Hoelterhoff, Rosita Sarnoff und Tony Randall beim Empfang vor dem 16. Piscator Preis am 2. April 2003 im Lotos Club (v.l.n.r.)

4 Sopran Licia Albanese, Dr. Robert J. Campbell und Edna Lind (v.r.n.l.)

5 Marina Kellen French (right) with Gisela von der Planitz (left) and Robert H. Mundheim

6 Gathered for the group photo are (from left): Robert H. Mundheim, Heather Randall, Stephen and Anna-Maria Kellen, Michael Lahr, Tony Randall, John W. Simmons, Anna Moffo, Gregorij von Leïtis, Felicitas Viermetz, Peter Clark, Kurt F. Viermetz, and Bernhard von der Planitz

7 Carol Kahn Strauss, Pierre van Goethem, Louise Kerz Hirschfeld, Dr. Christoph Thun-Hohenstein, and Baroness Mariuccia Zerilli Marimo (from left)

8 Anna Moffo (left) accepts the Piscator Award from Gregorij von Leïtis

5 Marina Kellen French (rechts) mit Gisela von der Planitz (links) und Robert H. Mundheim

6 Zum Gruppenphoto versammelten sich (v.l.n.r.) Robert H. Mundheim, Heather Randall, Stephen und Anna-Maria Kellen, Michael Lahr, Tony Randall, John W. Simmons, Anna Moffo, Gregorij von Leïtis, Felicitas Viermetz, Peter Clark, Kurt F. Viermetz und Bernhard von der Planitz

7 Carol Kahn Strauss, Pierre van Goethem, Louise Kerz Hirschfeld, Dr. Christoph Thun-Hohenstein und Baronin Mariuccia Zerilli Marimo (v.l.n.r.)

8 Anna Moffo nimmt den Piscator Preis aus den Händen von Gregorij von Leïtis entgegen

2004

Kitty Carlisle Hart

Piscator Award, American Singer, Actress, and Spokeswoman for the Arts, 1910 – 2007
Piscator Preis, Amerikanische Sängerin, Schauspielerin und Verfechterin der Künste, 1910 – 2007

Kitty Carlisle Hart's first Broadway appearance was in *Champagne Sec*. In the world of opera, she created the role of Lucretia in the American premiere of Benjamin Britten's *The Rape of Lucretia*. She made her debut at the Metropolitan Opera in 1967 as Prince Orlofsky in *Die Fledermaus*.

Her film appearances include a starring role in the Marx Brothers' classic, *A Night at the Opera*, two films with Bing Crosby, *She Loves Me Not*, and *Here is My Heart*, and later, roles in Woody Allen's *Radio Days* and in the film version of *Six Degrees of Separation*. For 15 years she was a regular panelist on the TV show *To Tell The Truth*.

Kitty Carlisle Hart was Chairperson Emeritus of the New York State Council on the Arts, having served from 1976 until 1996.
Her concern for women's role in society led to her appointment as chairperson of the Statewide Conference of Women and later as special consultant to Governor Nelson Rockefeller on Women's Opportunities. In 1991 President George Bush presented her with the National Medal of Arts.

Am Broadway trat Kitty Carlisle Hart zuerst auf in *Champagne Sec*. In der US-Erstaufführung von Benjamin Brittens Oper *The Rape of Lucretia* sang sie die Titelrolle. 1967 hatte sie ihr Debüt an der Metropolitan Opera als Prinz Orlofsky in *Die Fledermaus*.

In dem Filmklassiker *Skandal in der Oper* mit den Marx Brothers hatte sie eine Hauptrolle, spielte in zwei Filmen mit Bing Crosby – *She Loves Me Not* und *Here Is My Heart* – und später in Woody Allens *Radio Days*, sowie in der Verfilmung von John Guares Stück *Das Leben – Ein Sechserpack*. 15 Jahre lang wirkte sie in der Fernseh-Show *To Tell The Truth* mit.

Von 1976 bis 1996 wirkte Kitty Carlisle Hart als Vorsitzende des Kunstausschusses des Staates New York. Ihr besonderes Interesse galt der Rolle der Frau in der Gesellschaft. Sie war Vorsitzende der New Yorker Frauenkonferenz und wurde später von Gouverneur Nelson Rockefeller zur Beraterin in Frauenfragen ernannt. 1991 erhielt sie von Präsident George Bush die National Medal of Arts.

Dr. Johann Georg Prinz von Hohenzollern

Honorary Piscator Award, German Cultural Manager and Patron of the Arts, born 1932
Piscator Ehrenpreis, Deutscher Kulturmanager und Kunstförderer, geboren 1932

After having studied art history and classical archaeology in Paris and Munich, Dr. Johann Georg Prince of Hohenzollern began working as a curator. From 1985 until 1992 he was General Director of the Bavarian National Museum. During his tenure the museum acquired the art collection of Fritz Thyssen. In 1992 he became General Director of the Bavarian State Picture Collection. From 1998 until 2006 he was Director of the Exhibition Hall of the Hypo Cultural Foundation. For several years he chaired the council of the Foundation of the Pinakothek der Moderne in Munich.

As a curator and cultural manager he helped stage a number of highly successful art exhibitions, such as *René Lalique, Carl Fabergé*, the *Art of the Medici*, and *Madame de Pompadour*.

He is one of the founding members and president of the Concert Society Munich, supporting young talented artists, international cultural exchange and the Munich Bach and Mozart concert series.

Nach dem Studium der Kunstgeschichte und Archäologie in Paris und München, arbeitete Dr. Johann Georg Prinz von Hohenzollern zunächst als Konservator und schließlich Landeskonservator. Von 1985 bis 1992 war er Generaldirektor des Bayerischen Nationalmuseums. Unter seiner Leitung erwarb das Museum die Kunstsammlung von Fritz Thyssen. 1992 wechselte er als Generaldirektor an die Bayerischen Staatsgemäldesammlungen. Von 1998 bis 2006 war er Direktor der Kunsthalle der Hypo-Kulturstiftung. Viele Jahre arbeitete er außerdem als Vorsitzender des Stiftungsrates der Stiftung Pinakothek der Moderne.

Als Ausstellungsmacher hat er etliche sehr erfolgreiche Großausstellungen konzipiert, u.a. *René Lalique, Carl Fabergé, Die Kunst der Medici*, und *Madame de Pompadour*.

Er ist Gründungsmitglied und Präsident der Konzertgesellschaft München e.V., deren Hauptanliegen die künstlerische Nachwuchsförderung, der internationale Kulturaustausch und die Förderung der Münchner Bach und Mozart Konzerte ist.

1 Kitty Carlisle Hart signs the Elysium guest book on March 24, 2004

2 The former Cultural Commissioner of New York City, Schuyler G. Chapin (2nd from right), who spoke about Kitty Carlisle Hart, and his wife Catia (center) are welcomed by Michael Lahr at their arrival at the Lotos Club

3 Renate Oldoerp, Margaret J. Leytess-Hoffman, Kathleen A. Moskal and her husband Robert R. McCord, and Sigrid Fischer (from left)

4 Uwe Karsten Heye (left), then the German Consul General in New York, reads a message of greeting of the German Chancellor Gerhard Schröder

1 Kitty Carlisle Hart trägt sich am 24. März 2004 ins Gästebuch von Elysium ein

2 Der frühere New Yorker Kulturdezernent Schuyler G. Chapin (2.v.r.), der die Laudatio auf Kitty Carlisle Hart hielt, und dessen Frau Catia (Mitte) werden bei ihrer Ankunft im Lotos Club von Michael Lahr begrüßt

3 Renate Oldoerp, Margaret J. Leytess-Hoffman, Kathleen A. Moskal mit ihrem Mann Robert R. McCord und Sigrid Fischer (v.l.n.r.)

4 Uwe Karsten Heye (links), damaliger deutscher Generalkonsul in New York, verliest eine Grußbotschaft des deutschen Bundeskanzlers Gerhard Schröder

5

6

7

10

8

9

5 Edith von Bohlen und Halbach (left) and the Munich gallery owner Carol Johnssen arrive at castle Höhenried on the shores of lake Starnberg for the presentation of the Honorary Piscator Award on July 4, 2004.

6 Prof. Gabriele Henkel (center) in conversation with Dr. Johann Georg Prince of Hohenzollern (left), and Gregorij von Leïtis

7 Dr. Christine Gräfin Esterhazy (center) talks with Kurt F. Viermetz. In the foreground left: Felicitas Viermetz

8 Dr. Johann Georg Prince of Hohenzollern (right) shows the Honorary Piscator Award Certificate in the presence of Leon Askin, Austrian exiled actor and collaborator of Piscator, and Gregorij von Leïtis

9 Gregorij von Leïtis, Leopoldine Countess Arco-Valley-Stengel, and the Chairman of the Board of the German Branch of Elysium – between two continents, Clemens von Schoeler (from left) during a raffle, which took place after the Award Ceremony during a festive lunch at the Bernried monastery

10 Eckbert von Bohlen und Halbach, Bernried's Mayor Josef Steigenberger, Leon Askin, Dr. Johann Georg Prince of Hohenzollern, and Kurt F. Viermetz, who introduced the honoree (from left)

5 Edith von Bohlen und Halbach (links) und die Münchner Galeristin Carol Johnssen bei der Ankunft zur Verleihung des Piscator Ehrenpreises am 4. Juli 2004 in Schloß Höhenried am Starnberger See

6 Prof. Gabriele Henkel (Mitte) im Gespräch mit Dr. Johann Georg Prinz von Hohenzollern (links) und Gregorij von Leïtis

7 Dr. Christine Gräfin Esterhazy (Mitte) unterhält sich mit Kurt F. Viermetz. Im Vordergrund links Felicitas Viermetz

8 Dr. Johann Georg Prinz von Hohenzollern (rechts) präsentiert die Piscator Ehrenpreis-Urkunde im Beisein des österreichischen Exil-Schauspielers und Piscator-Mitarbeiters Leon Askin (sitzend) und Gregorij von Leïtis

9 Gregorij von Leïtis, Leopoldine Gräfin von Arco-Valley-Stengel und der Vorsitzende von Elysium – between two continents e.V. Clemens von Schoeler (v.l.n.r.) bei der Tombola, die im Anschluß an die Preisverleihung beim festlichen Essen im Kloster Bernried stattfindet

10 Eckbert von Bohlen und Halbach, Bernrieds Bürgermeister Josef Steigenberger, Leon Askin, Dr. Johann Georg Prinz von Hohenzollern und Laudator Kurt F. Viermetz (v.l.n.r.)

» Especially today, the great Independence Day in the U.S., the 228th, thoughts turn to the challenges of these days, and the responsibilities on both sides in these difficult times. I am glad that as a German, a former resident of New York and now of Munich, I have always supported and followed Elysium's activities – in good and in difficult times. And I'm proud that I was honored a few years ago with this Piscator Award.

But this is the hour of our friend Dr. Johann Georg Prince of Hohenzollern.

He is being honored for his support of art and culture in memory of last century's great theatrical producer Piscator in his New York and Berlin years. Furtherance of art and culture, support for all kinds of initiatives in this large and important area in every society is not necessarily a matter of course, especially not in Germany. In USA – as we all know – that is part of daily life, "it's a way of life". A propos, the other day I read a commentary in one of the leading American newspapers about this important social responsibility. It was headlined: "Charity and cultural support is good – but we can do much better!" And exactly for that reason the achievements and activities of the Prince of Hohenzollern are so extraordinary, especially in our German society and, rightfully, they had to be honored, as is the case today, as Elysium has decided.

Our Prince, if I may be so bold as to formulate this so colloquially, is a super-human being and a super talent. He is, first of all, a human being with a warm heart and, I would say, one equipped with absolute humanity. Big or small, rich or poor, famous or modest, whoever knocks at his door, the Prince understands how to excite people, how to motivate them with humor and with his decidedly easy-going way, and to get them to go along.

As I see it, his life can be defined in two ways: a career at the Central Institute for Art History in Munich; curator, and later director general at the Bavarian State Collection of Paintings; director general of the Bavarian National Museum, and chairman of the board of the Hypokulturstiftung (Hypobank Cultural Foundation). It shows his extraordinary talent at the top of the world of art and painting in Germany's culture capital Munich.

The other definition, ladies and gentlemen, is that of the grand seigneur, who is fond of the beautiful things of this world, of music, of art, of beautiful creatures, of nature, of cultural travel.

Our Prince is famous for his commitment to the Concert Society of Munich and for his successful pleading for financial support for the Bavarian state museums. There are really very few people south of the River Main who better fit the profile of a supporter of art and culture in our society than our Prince of Hohenzollern. «

Kurt F. Viermetz
Excerpts from his remarks on Dr. Johann Georg Prince of Hohenzollern

Translation: Christine Schurtman

110

» Gerade heute, am großen Unabhängigkeitstag der Vereinigten Staaten, dem 228., wandern unsere Gedanken in die Richtung der Herausforderungen in diesen Tagen und der Verantwortungen auf beiden Seiten in dieser schwierigen Zeit. Ich freue mich als Deutscher, früher in New York und jetzt in München ansässig, immer die Aktivitäten von Elysium unterstützt und begleitet zu haben – in guten und in schwierigen Tagen. Und ich bin stolz darauf, auch vor einigen Jahren mit dieser Piscator-Auszeichnung geehrt worden zu sein.

Dies ist aber die Stunde unseres Freundes, Dr. Johann Georg Prinz von Hohenzollern!

Er wird ausgezeichnet für die Förderung von Kunst und Kultur in Erinnerung an den großartigen Theatermacher Piscator der Berliner und New Yorker Jahre im vergangenen Jahrhundert. Förderung von Kunst und Kultur, Unterstützung aller möglichen Initiativen in diesem weiten und wichtigen Bereich jeder Gesellschaft ist bei weitem nicht selbstverständlich, schon gar nicht heute und schon gar nicht in Deutschland. In den USA – wie wir alle wissen – gehört das zum täglichen Leben, „its a way of life". A propos: Neulich las ich in einer führenden amerikanischen Zeitung einen Kommentar über diese wichtige gesellschaftliche Verantwortung mit der ganz einfachen Überschrift: „Charity and cultural support is good – but we can do much better!" Und genau aus diesem Grunde ist Leistung und Aktivität des Prinzen von Hohenzollern so außergewöhnlich, gerade in unserer deutschen Gesellschaft, und musste zu Recht gewürdigt werden, wie das heute der Fall ist, wie Elysium es entschieden hat.

Unser Prinz – wenn ich mir erlauben darf, das so volkstümlich zu formulieren – ist ein Super-Mensch und ein Super-Talent. Er ist, erstens ein Mensch mit Herzenswärme, ich würde sagen mit ausgesprochener Menschlichkeit versehen.

Ob groß oder klein, reich oder arm, berühmt oder bescheiden, - wer immer bei ihm anklopft, er, der Prinz, versteht es, Menschen zu begeistern, sie mit Humor und seiner ausgesprochen lockeren Art zu motivieren, mitzumachen.

Sein Leben kann man aus meiner Sicht auf zweierlei Art definieren: Karriere im Zentralinstitut für Kunstgeschichte in München, Konservator und später Generaldirektor an den Bayerischen Staatsgemäldesammlungen, Generaldirektor des Bayerischen Nationalmuseums, Vorstandsvorsitzender der HypoKulturstiftung. Sie zeigt das großartige Talent an der Spitze der Welt der Kunst und Malerei in Deutschlands Kulturhauptstadt München.

Die andere Definition, meine Damen und Herren, ist die eines Grandseigneurs, der den schönen Dingen dieser Welt zugetan ist: der Musik, der Kunst, unseren schönen Geschöpfen, der Natur, den bildenden Reisen.

Unser Prinz ist berühmt für sein Engagement für die Konzertgesellschaft München, für das erfolgreiche Betteln um finanzielle Unterstützung der Staatlichen Museen Bayerns. Es gibt südlich der Mainlinie wirklich nicht viele, die besser in das Profil der Förderung von Kunst und Kultur in unserer Gesellschaft passen, als unser Prinz von Hohenzollern. «

Kurt F. Viermetz
Auszug aus seiner Laudatio auf Dr. Johann Georg Prinz von Hohenzollern

2005

Ben Gazzara

Piscator Award, American Actor, 1930 – 2012
Piscator Preis, Amerikanischer Schauspieler, 1930 – 2012

Ben Gazzara studied at Erwin Piscator's Dramatic Workshop and was a member of the Actors Studio in its first and most memorable years. Years later he remarked that the discovery of his love for acting saved him from a life of crime during his teen years. He made his mark on the stage and with the New York critics in his theatrical debut as Jocko de Paris in *End As A Man*, which became his first film retitled *The Strange One*, both directed by Jack Garfein.

His work in the theater included roles in Elia Kazan's production of *Cat on a Hot Tin Roof*, *A Hatful of Rain* directed by Frank Corsaro, and *Who's Afraid of Virginia Woolf?* directed by Edward Albee himself. On the big screen, Gazzara created some of his most formidable characters in collaboration with his friend John Cassavetes in the movies *Husbands*, *Killing of a Chinese Bookie*, and *Opening Night*. His collaboration with Peter Bogdanovich produced *Saint Jack* and *They All Laughed*. Among his numerous other films were Otto Preminger's *Anatomy of a Murder*, David Mamet's *The Spanish Prisoner,* and Lars von Trier's *Dogville*.

Ben Gazzara studierte in Piscators Dramatic Workshop und war Mitglied im Actors Studio in den denkwürdigen Anfangsjahren. Später sagte er, dass die Entdeckung seiner Liebe zum Schauspiel ihn während seiner Jugend vor dem Abrutschen in die Kriminalität bewahrt habe. Er profilierte sich bei den Zuschauern und New Yorker Kritikern mit seinem Theaterdebüt als Jocko de Paris in *Stirb wie ein Mann*. Er spielte dieselbe Rolle auch in der Verfilmung, die wie das Stück von Jack Garfein inszeniert wurde.

Des weiteren wirkte er mit in Elia Kazans Produktion von *Die Katze auf dem heißen Blechdach*, in Frank Corsaros *Giftiger Schnee* und in *Wer hat Angst vor Virginia Woolf?* inszeniert vom Autor Edward Albee selbst. Auf der Kinoleinwand schuf Gazzara einige seiner denkwürdigsten Charaktere mit dem Filmemacher John Cassavetes in *Ehemänner*, *Die Ermordung eines chinesischen Buchmachers* und *Opening Night*. Unter Peter Bogdanovichs Regie entstanden *Saint Jack* und *Sie haben alle gelacht*. Außerdem spielte er in Otto Premingers *Anatomie eines Mordes*, in David Mamets *Die unsichtbare Falle* und in Lars von Triers *Dogville*.

Donald M. Kendall

Honorary Piscator Award, American Business Executive and Philanthropist, born 1921
Piscator Ehrenpreis, Amerikanischer Geschäftsmann und Mäzen, geboren 1921

Donald M. Kendall is co-founder of PepsiCo and was its Chief Executive Officer for 21 years until his retirement in 1986. A National Business Hall of Fame laureate, Kendall has been recognized as one of the giants of American industry. Not only did he build one of the world's premier consumer products companies, he also used his position in business to advance the cause of international understanding and to promote human equality and justice.

Kendall was active in the US-USSR Trade and Economic Council, the Chamber of Commerce of the United States and served as chairman of the board of the American Ballet Theatre foundation.

When PepsiCo moved its headquarters from Manhattan to a site in suburban Purchase, Donald Kendall initiated the creation of the Donald M. Kendall Sculpture Gardens, an outstanding collection of 20th century outdoor sculpture that can be enjoyed by the employees, the community and the public. Kendall himself selected the sculptures.

Donald M. Kendall ist Mitgründer von PepsiCo und war bis zu seinem Ausscheiden 1986 21 Jahre lang dessen Vorstandsvorsitzender. Als Mitglied der National Business Hall of Fame gilt Kendall als einer der Giganten der amerikanischen Industrie. Er baute nicht nur eines der weltgrößten Konsumgüterunternehmen auf, er nutzte seine Stellung auch, um internationale Verständigung, Gleichberechtigung und Gerechtigkeit zu fördern.

Kendall war aktives Mitglied des Amerikanisch-Russischen Handels- und Wirtschaftsrates, der US-Handelskammer und Vorstand der Stiftung des American Ballet Theatre.

Als PepsiCo seinen Firmensitz aus Manhattan ins vorstädtische Purchase verlegte, initiierte Kendall die Schaffung des Donald M. Kendall Skulpturengartens. An der herausragenden Sammlung von Freilandskulpturen des 20. Jahrhunderts können sich die Firmenmitarbeiter, die Anwohner und die allgemeine Öffentlichkeit erfreuen. Kendall selbst suchte alle Skulpturen aus.

1 Scott Krawitz, Gregorij von Leïtis, and Karin Martin at the 18th Annual Erwin Piscator Award Luncheon on February 22, 2005 at the Lotos Club (from left)

2 Gregorij von Leïtis (left) with the long-time director of the Guggenheim Museum Dr. Thomas M. Messer, who served as a member of the advisory board of Elysium and The Lahr von Leïtis Academy & Archive until his death in 2013

3 Uwe Karsten Heye (left), and Sabine Haack

4 Eli Wallach, Kitty Carlisle Hart, Ben and Elke Gazzara (from left)

1 Scott Krawitz, Gregorij von Leïtis und Karin Martin bei der 18. Piscator Preisverleihung am 22. Februar 2005 im Lotos Club (v.l.n.r.)

2 Gregorij von Leïtis (links) mit dem langjährigen Direktor des Guggenheim-Museums Dr. Thomas M. Messer, der bis zu seinem Tod 2013 Kuratoriums-Mitglied von Elysium und The Lahr von Leïtis Academy & Archive war

3 Uwe Karsten Heye (links) und Sabine Haack

4 Eli Wallach, Kitty Carlisle Hart, Ben und Elke Gazzara (v.l.n.r.)

5 Paola Munzi, Deputy Consul General of Italy in New York, Ben Gazzara and Jolana Blau, who was the Chairperson of the Piscator Luncheon Committee from 2005 until 2007 (from left)

6 Joy Ferro, Felicie Balay, Dr. Christoph Thun-Hohenstein, and Roberta Glenn (from left)

7 William Hetzler (left) hands a copy of the message of greeting by New York's Governor George E. Pataki to Jacqueline Millen (right), who accepted the Honorary Piscator Award 2005 on behalf of Donald M. Kendall

8 Sabine Haack, Michael Lahr and Gregorij von Leïtis applaud the Piscator Award recipient of 2005, Ben Gazzara (from left)

5 Paola Munzi, stellvertretende italienische Generalkonsulin in New York, Ben Gazzara und Jolana Blau, die von 2005 bis 2007 den Vorsitz des Piscator Luncheon Komitees führte (v.l.n.r.)

6 Joy Ferro, Felicie Balay, Dr. Christoph Thun-Hohenstein und Roberta Glenn (v.l.n.r)

7 William Hetzler (links) überreicht eine Kopie der Grußbotschaft von New Yorks Gouverneur George E. Pataki an Jacqueline Millen (rechts), die in Vertretung von Donald M. Kendall den Ehrenpreis 2005 entgegennimmt

8 Sabine Haack, Michael Lahr und Gregorij von Leïtis applaudieren dem Piscator Preisträger 2005 Ben Gazzara (v.l.n.r.)

2006

Elaine Stritch

Piscator Award, American Actress and Vocalist, born 1925
Piscator Preis, Amerikanische Schauspielerin und Sängerin, geboren 1925

Elaine Stritch studied with Erwin Piscator at his Dramatic Workshop at the New School. Other students at this time included Marlon Brando and Bea Arthur. Beginning her career in musical comedy on Broadway, she went from standing by for Ethel Merman in *Call Me Madam* to her Tony-nominated performance in the revival of Albee's *A Delicate Balance*. Among her many Broadway credits are *Angel in the Wings*, *On Your Toes*, *Bus Stop* and *Sail Away*. In London's West End she starred in Neil Simon's *The Gingerbread Lady* and Tennessee Williams' *Small Craft Warnings*.

Stritch made her film debut in the 1957 remake of *A Farewell to Arms*. She starred in Alain Resnais' film *Providence*, in Woody Allen's films *September* and *Small Time Crooks*, and played Winona Ryder's loving grandmother in *Autumn in New York*.

She won a Tony Award for the Broadway production of *Elaine Stritch at Liberty*, a biting, hilarious, touching tour-de-force tour of her life and career, talking candidly about her dates with Marlon Brando, Ben Gazzara and Rock Hudson and her long battle with alcohol.

Elaine Stritch studierte mit Erwin Piscator; ihre Mitstudenten am Dramatic Workshop waren Marlon Brando und Bea Arthur. Sie begann ihre Broadway-Laufbahn als Zweitbesetzung für Ethel Merman im Musical *Call Me Madam*. Für ihre Rolle in Albees *Ein empfindliches Gleichgewicht* wurde sie 1996 für den Tony nominiert. Andere Broadway-Erfolge sind: *Angel in the Wings*, *On Your Toes*, *Bus Stop* und *Sail Away*. Im Londoner Westend spielte sie die Hauptrollen in Neil Simons *The Gingerbread Lady* und Tennessee Williams *Small Craft Warnings*.

Stritch hatte ihr Filmdebüt 1957 im Remake von *In einem anderen Land*. Sie spielte in Alain Resnais' Film *Providence*, in Woody Allens Filmen *September* und *Schmalspurganoven*, und verkörperte die liebende Großmutter von Winona Ryder in *Es begann im September*.

Sie gewann den Tony für ihr Broadway-Stück *Elaine Stritch at Liberty*, eine bissige, witzige, berührende und bravouröse Rückschau auf ihr Leben. Darin erzählt sie aufrichtig von ihren Rendezvous mit Marlon Brando, Ben Gazzara und Rock Hudson und von ihrem jahrelangen Kampf mit dem Alkohol.

Gary Hattem

Honorary Piscator Award, American President of Deutsche Bank Americas Foundation
Piscator Ehrenpreis, Amerikanischer Präsident der Deutsche Bank Americas Foundation

Gary Hattem, who holds a Masters Degree in City and Regional Planning from Pratt Institute, is President of Deutsche Bank Americas Foundation and manages the bank's philanthropic program with grants made in the fields of education, arts and the environment, as well as community development.

In the United States, Latin America, and Canada, the Deutsche Bank Americas Foundation and DB Community Development Finance Group carry out the Bank's corporate citizenship commitments through a strategic program of loans, investments and philanthropic grants targeted to assist communities that are in the process of revitalization. The Bank has consistently earned "outstanding" Community Reinvestment Act ratings for its role in providing capital to low- and moderate-income communities. These activities have positioned Deutsche Bank as a pioneering force in addressing social needs – with innovative ideas, dedicated leaderhip and creative partnership-building efforts.

The Bank also supports projects that promote the arts, cross-cultural initiatives and education.

Gary Hattem, der einen Magister in Stadt- und Raumplanung hat, ist Präsident der Deutsche Bank Americas Stiftung und leitet das philanthropische Programm der Bank. Die Stiftung unterstützt Bildung, Kunst, Umweltschutz und die Entwicklung des Gemeinwesens.

In den USA, Lateinamerika und Kanada erfüllt die Stiftung zusammen mit der DB Community Development Finance Group den Auftrag des bürgerschaftlichen Engagements der Bank. Durch strategische Kredite, Investments und Fördermittel hilft sie Gemeinwesen, die im Prozeß der Revitalisierung begriffen sind. Das Bereitstellen von Kapital an Bevölkerungsgruppen mit niedrigem und mäßigem Einkommen seitens der Bank wird durchweg positiv bewertet. Dank ihrer Aktivitäten auf diesem Gebiet gilt die Deutsche Bank als Pionier, wenn es darum geht, soziale Nöte mit innovativen Ideen, Engagement und kreativen langfristigen Partnerschaften zu bekämpfen.

Die amerikanische Stiftung der Deutschen Bank unterstützt ebenso Projekte der Kunstförderung, interkulturelle Initiativen und Bildungsmaßnahmen.

1 Stephen M. Harnik (left) and the Austrian Consul General Dr. Brigitta Blaha at the 19th Piscator Award Ceremony on February 15, 2006

2 Stefan Hemmerle (right) greets Helen Doctorow (2nd from left) and Jolana Blau (center); Christian Hemmerle is visible on the left side of the picture

3 Between the various speeches and courses of the festive menu, Stephen M. Harnik, Elaine Stritch, Gregorij von Leïtis, and Anna Moffo chat with one another in the ball room of the Lotos Club (from left)

4 Elaine Stritch (standing at the lectern) tells the audience how much Erwin Piscator has influenced her and shares anecdotes of her time at the Dramatic Workshop, where Marlon Brando was one of her co-students. At the end she confesses: "I have received many honors like this and they all mean something to me. But this one means everything to me."

1 Stephen M. Harnik (links) und die österreichische Generalkonsulin Dr. Brigitta Blaha beim 19. Piscator Preis am 15. Februar 2006

2 Stefan Hemmerle (rechts) begrüßt Helen Doctorow (2.v.l.) und Jolana Blau (Mitte); links im Bild Christian Hemmerle

3 Zwischen den Reden und den einzelnen Gängen des Festmenüs plaudern Stephen M. Harnik, Elaine Stritch, Gregorij von Leïtis und Anna Moffo im Ballsaal des Lotos Clubs miteinander (v.l.n.r.)

4 Elaine Stritch (stehend am Rednerpult) erzählt in ihrer Dankrede, wie sehr Piscator sie geprägt hat und gibt Anekdoten aus ihrer Zeit am Dramatic Workshop zum besten, wo sie gemeinsam mit Marlon Brando studiert hat. Zum Schluß sagt sie: "Ich habe viele Ehrungen erhalten, und sie bedeuten mir alle etwas, doch dieser Preis bedeutet mir alles."

» The 19th century Swiss writer Gottfried Keller once reminded his grumbling contemporaries that it would be far "healthier to hope nothing but to realize that which is possible, instead of dreaming and not doing anything." Indeed, I believe this to be the most noble and important task of corporate and private philanthropy: to assist in the creation and realization of the possible while at the same time encouraging and fostering the search for solutions to the seemingly impossible. Enlightened philanthropy – as I would call it – is actively involved, is inventive; it is not content with just signing checks and haphazard charitable giving.

Enlightened philanthropy combines patience and far-sightedness with the duty to take risks. The results of such informed and imaginative beneficence are adventurous initiatives that seek positive change – change which often surpasses the capacity of governments. Those enlightened and inventive philanthropists serve as catalysts, they are visionaries[...] Those enlightened philanthropists promote ideas.

Deutsche Bank Americas Foundation represents this ideal of enlightened philanthropy in an exemplary way. With a worldwide presence, Deutsche Bank is simultaneously a global corporate citizen, yet deeply rooted in the many local communities where it operates. [...]

I just said that enlightened philanthropists promote ideas. The idea – which to me seems at the core of all the activities of Deutsche Bank Americas Foundation – is: Helping people to help themselves! «

Michael Lahr
Excerpts from his remarks on the Deutsche Bank Americas Foundation

» Der Schweizer Schriftsteller Gottfried Keller rief seinen mürrischen Zeitgenossen im 19. Jahrhundert in Erinnerung: „Es ist gesünder, nichts zu hoffen und das Mögliche zu schaffen, als zu schwärmen und nichts zu tun." In der Tat bin ich davon überzeugt, dass dies die nobelste und wichtigste Aufgabe betrieblicher und privater Philanthropie ist: Bei der Verwirklichung des Möglichen zu assistieren und gleichzeitig die Suche nach Lösungen für das scheinbar Unmögliche zu ermutigen und zu unterstützen. Aufgeklärte Philanthropie – wie ich es nennen möchte – ist aktiv beteiligt, ist erfinderisch, gibt sich nicht zufrieden mit dem Ausstellen von Schecks und planlosen mildtätigen Spenden.

Aufgeklärte Philanthropie vereint Geduld und Weitsichtigkeit mit der Pflicht Risiken einzugehen. Das Ergebnis solcher sachkundigen und erfinderischen Wohltätigkeit sind experimentierfreudige Initiativen, die positiven Wandel anstreben – Wandel, der die Möglichkeiten von Regierungen oft übertrifft. Diese aufgeklärten und einfallsreichen Philanthropen fungieren als Katalysatoren, sie sind Visionäre [...] Diese aufgeklärten Mäzene fördern Ideen.

Deutsche Bank Americas Foundation ist ein mustergültiges Beispiel für das Ideal aufgeklärter Philanthropie. Mit ihrer weltweiten Präsenz ist die Deutsche Bank gleichzeitig ein unternehmerischer Weltbürger, und doch tief verwurzelt in den vielen örtlichen Gemeinschaften, in denen sie tätig ist. [...]

Ich sagte gerade, dass aufgeklärte Philanthropen Ideen fördern. Die Idee – die meiner Meinung nach den Kern aller Aktivitäten der Deutsche Bank Americas Foundation ausmacht – ist: Hilfe zur Selbsthilfe! «

Michael Lahr
Auszug aus seiner Laudatio auf die Deutsche Bank Americas Foundation

2007

Deborah Voigt

Piscator Award, American Dramatic Soprano and "down-to-earth Diva", born 1960
Piscator Preis, Amerikanische dramatische Sopranistin und „bodenständige Diva", geboren 1960

Deborah Voigt known to her twitter fans as "down-to-earth diva", is one of today's greatest interpreters of dramatic opera roles by Richard Strauss and Richard Wagner. She has given definitive performances of Ariadne, Salome, Kaiserin in *Frau ohne Schatten* and Chrysothemis in *Elektra*, as well as Sieglinde in *Die Walküre*, Elisabeth in *Tannhäuser,* and Isolde. She also enjoys great acclaim in such popular Italian roles as Tosca, Aida, Leonore in *La Forza Del Destino* and Amelia in *Un Ballo In Maschera*, a role she sang in her Metropolitan Opera debut in 1991. In addition, she is active as a recitalist and has given several performances of popular fare and Broadway standards, including benefit concerts for Broadway Cares / Equity Fights AIDS and the New York Theatre Workshop.

Voigt's extensive discography includes two popular solo recordings, *All My Heart* and *Obsessions*.

She recently set up the Deborah Voigt / Vero Beach Opera Foundation's Protégé Mentoring Program that includes voice and acting training.

Deborah Voigt, ihren Twitter-Fans bekannt als "bodenständige Diva", ist eine der führenden Interpretinnen dramatischer Opernrollen von Richard Strauss und Richard Wagner. Sie hat mit ihren Darbietungen von Ariadne, Salome, Kaiserin in *Frau ohne Schatten* und Chrysothemis in *Elektra* Maßstäbe gesetzt, ebenso wie mit Sieglinde in *Die Walküre*, Elisabeth im *Tannhäuser* und Isolde. Viel bejubelt sind auch ihre Darstellungen italienischer Rollen, von Tosca, bis zu Aida, Leonore in *La Forza Del Destino* und Amelia in *Un Ballo In Maschera,* ein Part, mit dem sie 1991 ihr Debüt an der Met gab. Außerdem singt sie häufig Konzerte mit populären und Broadway-Melodien, u.a. als Benefiz-Veranstaltungen für Broadway Cares / Equity Fights AIDS und den New York Theatre Workshop.

Ihre umfangreiche Diskographie umfasst zwei beliebte Solo-Einspielungen, *All My Heart* und *Obsessions*.

Kürzlich gründete sie das Deborah Voigt / Vero Beach Opernstiftungs-Förderungsprogramm. Die Protégés erhalten Stimm- und Schauspieltraining.

Alexandra Kauka

Honorary Piscator Award, American Publisher and Philanthropist
Piscator Ehrenpreis, Amerikanische Verlegerin und Mäzenin

Born in Carinthia, Austria, Alexandra Kauka has been living in the United States since 1980. With her late husband Rolf Kauka – often referred to as the "German Walt Disney" for his invention of Fix & Foxi, Bussi Bär and many other comic figures – she ran Kauka Promedia, Inc., a successor organization to Kauka's Publishing Company. Since Rolf Kauka's death in 2000, until early in 2013, Alexandra Kauka ran the business alone.

She is an important philanthropist with a special focus on music. She serves as a board member of the Metropolitan Opera in New York, is a generous donor to the Salzburg Festival, and has supported Washington National Opera and Arizona Opera. Taking her tasks very seriously, she also supports cultural centers, hospitals and other charities. "Life was so favorable to me, it would not be right, not to help others!" is how Alexandra Kauka explains her efforts in this area. She gave part of the Chinquapin Plantation in Thomasville, where she lived until recently, as the first nature preserve to the State of Georgia.

In 2011 she married Sterling Morton Hamill.

Aus ihrer österreichischen Heimat Kärnten zog Alexandra Kauka 1980 in die USA. Mit ihrem verstorbenen Mann Rolf Kauka – wegen seiner Erfindungen von Fix & Foxi, Bussi Bär und anderen Comicfiguren oft der „deutsche Walt Disney" genannt – führte sie die Geschäfte von Kauka Promedia, Inc. Seit Rolf Kaukas Tod im Jahr 2000 war sie bis Anfang 2013 alleinverantwortlich als Verlegerin tätig.

Sie engagiert sich maßgeblich als Mäzenin, speziell auf dem Gebiet der Musik. Sie ist Vorstandsmitglied der Metropolitan Opera in New York, eine großzügige Förderin der Salzburger Festspiele, und hat die Washington National Opera und die Arizona Opera unterstützt. Auch Kulturzentren, Krankenhäuser und andere gemeinnützige Organisationen profitieren von ihrer Großzügigkeit. Sie nimmt ihr Mäzenatentum sehr ernst und erläutert ihre Haltung mit den Worten: „Das Leben war so gut zu mir, es wäre nicht richtig, anderen nicht zu helfen." Einen Teil der Chinquapin Plantage in Thomasville, wo sie bis vor kurzem wohnte, gab sie dem Staat Georgia als Naturschutzgebiet.

2011 heiratete sie Sterling Morton Hamill.

Marta Eggerth

Piscator Lifetime Achievement Award, Hungarian-American Singer, Actress and Legend, born 1912
Piscator Preis fürs Lebenswerk, Ungarisch-Amerikanische Sänger- und Schauspiellegende, geboren 1912

Born in Budapest, Marta Eggerth is often referred to as "the last of the Mohicans" as she is truly one of the last survivors of what is today often called "The Silver Age of Operetta". Many of the 20th century's most famous composers, including Franz Lehár, Emmerich Kálmán, Robert Stolz, and Paul Abraham, composed works especially for her. Her stage and film career began in her early teenage years. At age 17, she performed the role of Adele in Max Reinhardt's 1929 production of *Die Fledermaus*.

During the early 1930s she was discovered by the film industry. On the set of the 1934 film *My Heart is Calling You* she met the young Polish tenor, Jan Kiepura. They were married in 1936 and became known as Europe's Love Couple causing a sensation wherever they appeared. In 1938, they both emigrated to the United States. Together they starred on stages throughout America until Kiepura's premature death in 1966.

In 1998 she played an aging diva in the detective series, *Tatort*. In 1999, at age 87, Marta Eggerth sang on the stage of the Vienna State Opera marking the opera house's first production of Lehár's *The Merry Widow*.

Marta Eggerth, geboren in Budapest, wird oft als "die letzte Mohikanerin" bezeichnet, weil sie eine der ganz wenigen noch lebenden Personen ist, die das „Silberne Zeitalter der Operette" aktiv mitprägten. Viele berühmte Komponisten des 20. Jahrhunderts, darunter Franz Lehár, Emmerich Kálmán, Robert Stolz und Paul Abraham komponierten Werke eigens für sie. Ihre Bühnen- und Filmlaufbahn begann in ganz jungen Jahren. Mit 17 sang sie die Rolle der Adele in Max Reinhardts berühmter Inszenierung von *Die Fledermaus*.

Während der frühen 1930er Jahre wurde sie von der Filmindustrie entdeckt. 1934 lernte sie auf dem Set von *Mein Herz ruft nach Dir* den polnischen Tenor Jan Kiepura kennen. Sie heirateten 1936 und galten als das Traumpaar des europäischen Films. 1938 emigrierten beide in die Vereinigten Staaten. Dort standen sie oft gemeinsam auf der Bühne und gaben Konzerte bis zu Kiepuras viel zu frühem Tod im Jahre 1966.

1998 spielte Marta Eggerth eine alternde Diva in dem Tatort *Nie wieder Oper*. 1999 sang Eggerth im Alter von 87 Jahren Melodien aus Lehárs *Die lustige Witwe*. Anlaß war die erste Inszenierung dieser Operette auf der Bühne der Wiener Staatsoper.

1 Investment Banker and Philanthropist Henry H. Arnhold (left) with the long-time member the American Board of Directors of Elysium, Dr. Norbert Fischer (right), and Jan Storbeck

2 Alexandra Kauka (center), who was awarded the Honorary Piscator Award on February 15, 2007, with Isabelle Harnoncourt (left), and Gregorij von Leïtis

3 Shayne Doty, Peter Gelb, General Manager of the Metropolitan Opera who praised the achievements of Alexandra Kauka, Socrates Nicholas, Alexandra Kauka, and Sterling Morton Hamill (from left)

4 Alexandra Kauka with her son Markus Nolff and his wife Nina (from right)

1 Banker und Mäzen Henry H. Arnhold (links) mit dem langjährigen Mitglied des amerikanischen Board of Directors von Elysium Dr. Norbert Fischer (rechts) und Jan Storbeck

2 Alexandra Kauka (Mitte), die am 15. Februar 2007 den Piscator Ehrenpreis erhielt, mit Isabelle Harnoncourt (links) und Gregorij von Leïtis

3 Shayne Doty, Peter Gelb, der als General Manager der Metropolitan Opera die Laudatio auf Alexandra Kauka hielt, Socrates Nicholas, Alexandra Kauka und Sterling Morton Hamill (v.l.n.r.)

4 Alexandra Kauka mit ihrem Sohn Markus Nolff und dessen Frau Nina (v.r.n.l.)

5 Jack Doulin, Casting Director of the New York Theatre Workshop, who introduced Deborah Voigt, Piscator Award Recipient Deborah Voigt, Dr. Brigitta Blaha, Alexandra Kauka, Gregorij von Leïtis, Marta Eggerth, who received the first Piscator Lifetime Achievement Award, Heather Randall, who served as Chairwoman of the Luncheon Committee, and Michael Lahr (from right)

6 Lisa Salomon, Stanley Stangren, Jolana Blau, and Judith Natalucci (from left)

7 Marta Eggerth (center) with baritone Thomas Hampson (right), and Dr. Christoph Thun-Hohenstein, Director of the Austrian Cultural Forum New York, who introduced Marta Eggerth and her enormous artistic contributions

8 Pianist Marjan Kiepura (center), the son of Marta Eggerth and Jan Kiepura, with his wife Jane Knox (left), and Louise Kerz Hirschfeld

9 Jeannie Im (standing) sings the aria "How does a woman benefit from fidelity?" from Paul Abraham's operetta Ball im Savoy

5 Jack Doulin, der als Casting Director des New York Theatre Workshop die Ehrenrede auf Deborah Voigt hielt, Piscator Preisträgerin Deborah Voigt, Dr. Brigitta Blaha, Alexandra Kauka, Gregorij von Leïtis, Marta Eggerth, die für ihr Lebenswerk den 2007 erstmals vergebenen Piscator Lifetime Achievement Award erhielt, Heather Randall, Vorsitzende des Luncheon Komitees, und Michael Lahr (v.r.n.l.)

6 Lisa Salomon, Stanley Stangren, Jolana Blau und Judith Natalucci (v.l.n.r.)

7 Marta Eggerth (Mitte) mit dem Bariton Thomas Hampson (rechts) und Dr. Christoph Thun-Hohenstein, der als Direktor des Österreichischen Kulturforums in New York die Verdienste Marta Eggerths würdigte

8 Pianist Marjan Kiepura (Mitte), der Sohn von Marta Eggerth und Jan Kiepura, mit seiner Frau Jane Knox (links) und Louise Kerz Hirschfeld

9 Jeannie Im (stehend) singt zum Abschluß der Preisverleihungszeremonie „Was hat eine Frau von der Treue?" aus Paul Abrahams Operette Ball im Savoy

The Federal President
of the Republic of Austria

Heinz Fischer

Ladies and Gentlemen,

It is a great pleasure to have the opportunity to address you on the occasion of the 20th Erwin Piscator Award ceremony in New York.

Although in this day and age, great achievements of women in politics, science, and culture meet with recognition and great respect, this ceremonial gathering represents a particular highlight, as three outstanding ladies – Mrs. Voigt, Mrs. Kauka and Mrs. Eggerth – are being honored with an Erwin Piscator Award today. All three of them are most exceptional personalities who can point to great artistic achievements and undoubtedly fully deserve this prestigious award.

What they have in common, is their specific relationship to Austria and the fact that they are famous artists, each in her own métier. Their brilliance and dedication to their work as well as their untiring commitment have earned them greatest respect and admiration on both sides of the Atlantic.
As Federal President of the Republic of Austria I, therefore, take particular pride in congratulating them personally.

Mrs. Deborah Voigt receives the Erwin Piscator Award 2007, today. Se is a world-famous soprano and cherished guest at all great opera houses and has also repeatedly sung at the Vienna Opera. It is always a privilege to see her, and more importantly, to listen to her in Vienna. In addition, playing the title role in "The Love of Danae" gained her unforgettable success at the Salzburg Festival. I share her joy over the honor conferred on her.

. / .

The Erwin Piscator Honorary Award 2007 goes to the philanthropist Mrs. Alexandra Kauka. This prize is awarded in memory of another great Austrian - Maria Ley, wife of Erwin Piscator and choreographer at the Salzburg Festival under Max Reinhardt.

Mrs. Kauka, who was born in the southern Austrian Province of Carinthia, is a very remarkable lady, because of the unusual scope of her talents. Whether at the side of her famous husband Rolf Kauka or as independent artist and supporter of humanitarian and cultural projects, she has invariably displayed outstanding creative power. The Austrians take great pride in her who, as an American citizen, has become a truly cosmopolitan figure and we thank her for affirming her ties to Austria by financially supporting the Salzburg Festivals.

Finally, Mrs. Marta Eggerth who is honored with the Erwin Piscator Life Achievement Award today deserves utmost admiration.
Born in Budapest, the one-time infant prodigy developed a close relationship to Austria through her early voice lessons and engagements in Vienna. Her marriage to Jan Kiepura and their performances together as well as the many great movie roles she played have brought her international fame. Yet, she never forgot the city where she had received her early instruction as an artist, which she demonstrated in 1999, when, at the age of 87, she swept away the audience with a memorable performance at the Vienna Opera.

Ladies and Gentlemen,

I would also like to thank all of you who were involved in the selection of this year's award winners as well as all those who helped organize this event. There is no doubt that the memory of Erwin Piscator and his wife Maria Ley will always stay alive. I congratulate the award winners wholeheartedly and wish all the guests attending this festive ceremony a memorable day!

Grußwort des Bundespräsidenten der Republik Österreich
Dr. Heinz Fischer, 2007

Meine Damen und Herren!

Es macht mir große Freude, Ihnen anlässlich der Verleihung der Erwin Piscator Awards sehr herzliche Grüße und Wünsche in die Kulturmetropole New York zu übermitteln.

Selbst in einer Zeit, in der die schöpferischen Leistungen von Frauen in Politik, Wissenschaft und Kultur höchste Anerkennung und Bestätigung finden, ist das diesjährige Zusammentreffen der Ehrung dreier Frauen – Frau Deborah Voigt, Frau Alexandra Kauka und Frau Marta Eggerth – doch ein Höhepunkt der besonderen Art. Die diesjährigen Preisträgerinnen sind zweifellos ganz außergewöhnliche Persönlichkeiten mit vielschichtigen Leistungen, und sie sind deshalb in höchstem Maße würdig, mit diesem Preis ausgezeichnet zu werden.

Dazu kommt, dass alle drei zu Ehrenden in einer besonderen Beziehung zu meiner Heimat Österreich stehen. Alle drei sind in verschiedenster Weise als Künstlerinnen bekannt und berühmt geworden. Ihre Brillanz, ihre Hingabe an die Ziele ihres Schaffens und die Unermüdlichkeit ihres Engagements stößt dies- und jenseits des Atlantiks auf große Bewunderung. Als Bundespräsident der Republik Österreich ist es für mich eine große Freude, den Preisträgerinnen sehr herzlich zu gratulieren.

Deborah Voigt, weltberühmte Sopranistin, ist Gast an den großen Opernhäusern der Welt und auch der Wiener Staatsoper vielfach verbunden. Wir schätzen uns glücklich, sie immer wieder in Wien sehen und hören zu können. Auch bei den Salzburger Festspielen feierte sie mit der Titelpartie in *Die Liebe der Danae* einen unvergesslichen Erfolg. Ich freue mich mit ihr über den Erwin Piscator Award 2007.

Den Erwin Piscator Honorary Award 2007 erhält die Philanthropin Alexandra Kauka. Dieser Preis wird in Erinnerung an eine weitere große Österreicherin vergeben, nämlich Maria Ley, Ehefrau von Erwin Piscator und unter Max Reinhardt Choreographin bei den Salzburger Festspielen.

In Österreichs südlichem Bundesland Kärnten geboren, ist Alexandra Kauka allein durch eine ungewöhnliche Vielfalt an Begabungen eine bemerkenswerte Frau. Sowohl an der Seite ihres erfindungsreichen, weltbekannt gewordenen Gatten Rolf Kauka als auch als selbständige Künstlerin und Unterstützerin humanitärer und künstlerischer Projekte ist sie eine Persönlichkeit mit bewunderswerter Schaffenskraft. Die Österreicherinnen und Österreicher können auf Alexandra Kauka, die als

Amerikanerin Weltbürgerin geworden ist, in ganz besonderer Weise stolz sein. Darüber hinaus haben wir ihr ebenfalls zu danken, denn sie bekennt sich in ganz besonderer Weise zu Österreich durch die Förderung der Salzburger Festspiele.

Mit großer Bewunderung wende ich mich Frau Marta Eggerth zu, die heute durch den Erwin Piscator Life Achievement Award ausgezeichnet wird. In Budapest geboren, wurde das ehemalige „Wunderkind" durch eine frühe Gesangsausbildung und durch Engagements in Wien eng mit Österreich verbunden. Ihre Künstlerehe und ihr gemeinsames Auftreten mit Jan Kiepura, aber auch viele großartige Filmrollen brachten ihr internationale Berühmtheit ein. Dennoch gedachte sie immer auch der Stadt, der sie ihre frühe künstlerische Ausbildung verdankte. So stand sie 1999 im Alter von 87 Jahren auf der Bühne der Wiener Staatsoperr und riss die Zuschauer zu wahren Begeisterungsstürmen hin.

Meine Damen und Herren!

Ich danke allen, die sich um die Auswahl und die Begründung der Preisträgerinnen verdient gemacht haben, sowie all jenen, die diese Veranstaltung organisiert und geleitet haben. Im Hintergrund steht natürlich immer auch die wache Erinnerung an die geniale Persönlichkeit von Erwin Piscator und dessen österreichischer Frau Maria Ley.

Ich sende allen Gästen des 20. Erwin Piscator Award, allen voran den drei Preisträgerinnen, beste Grüße aus Wien und wünsche Ihnen allen eine gelungene Preisverleihung!

Heinz Fischer

Übersetzung: Österreichisches Bundespräsidialamt

» The Dramatic Workshop founded and run by Mr. and Mrs. Piscator at the New School for Social Research in 1939 was the immediate forerunner of what became the Actors Studio, and nurtured an esthetic that married a socially conscious theatre to a deeply personal acting style.

Each of the [past] recipients of this award has been an artist of the first rank, but each of them has also been a public figure who used her or his celebrity to enrich the world we live in.

I believe that Deborah Voigt is the youngest person to receive this award, and she seems an appropriate choice for this honor specifically because as an artist she brings such a human connection to the roles that she inhabits on the operatic stage and as a public figure she has taken her place in the public eye with grace, courage and an unpretentious simplicity.

For me, one of the best definitions of opera comes from a rather unlikely source, Lee Strasberg. He described opera as "not drama *with* music, but drama *in* music." Deborah Voigt's artistry is all about that. [...] She never tells a lie on stage. Because she brings a great deal of herself to the stage as only the greatest actors can do. «

Jack Doulin
Excerpts from his remarks on Deborah Voigt

» Congratulations, Deborah, on your Piscator Award. [...] Equally deserving of bravas is Alexandra Kauka, who is also being honored today with a Piscator Award. Alexandra is a less sung heroine of the Met, but without whom we would not be able to flourish. Alexandra is helping to save our art form through her enthusiastic patronage and support of the Met. [...]

She is also a star in her own right, which I discovered last summer when I arranged to meet her at the Salzburg Festival. While waiting for her in front of the Salzburg Festspielhaus in anticipation of a performance of *Figaro* starring Anna Netrebko, one of Alexandra's friends and favorite performers, I couldn't help but notice a gathering storm of paparazzi around the front of the theater. I assumed that they were waiting for the arrival of Netrebko. In fact, they were awaiting the arrival of Alexandra. «

Peter Gelb
Excerpts from his remarks on Alexandra Kauka

» Dear Marta Eggerth, what makes you so special? [...] Like Maria Callas in opera, nobody has gone as far as you have in operetta. When you sing operetta, your roles not only come alive but become larger than life!
[...] Opera tends to be on the tragic side of life and can be compared with red wine. Operetta is more like Champagne – sparkling in many ways [...] You think you know the difference – but actually you don't, if you have not heard Marta Eggerth. With her, Champagne suddenly has a heart, a heart full of emotion, and usually a lot of sex appeal.
[...] Dear Marta Eggerth, even if you are presented with a Life Achievement Award, it doesn't mean you can relax. [...] We all encourage you to pass your secret on to younger generations! Don't you hear the pleas of Lehár, Kálmán and many others who are passionately in love with you? «

Dr. Christoph Thun-Hohenstein
Excerpts from his remarks on Marta Eggerth

» Der Dramatic Workshop, 1939 an der New School for Social Research von Herrn und Frau Piscator gegründet und geleitet, war der direkte Vorläufer dessen, was später das Actors Studio wurde, und nährte eine Ästhetik, die ein sozial bewusstes Theater mit einem zutiefst persönlichen Schauspielstil vereinte.

Jeder der [früheren] Piscator Preisträger ist ein Künstler ersten Ranges, doch jeder ist zugleich auch eine Persönlichkeit des öffentlichen Lebens, die ihre Prominenz dazu nutzt, die Welt, in der wir leben, zu bereichern.

Soweit ich sehe, ist Deborah Voigt die bisher jüngste Empfängerin dieses Preises; sie scheint mir eine adäquate Wahl für diese Ehrung zu sein, besonders deshalb, weil sie als Künstlerin den Rollen, die sie auf der Opernbühne verkörpert, soviel Menschlichkeit verleiht. Als öffentliche Person füllt sie ihren Platz im Blickpunkt der Gesellschaft mit Anmut, Courage und unprätentiöser Einfachheit aus.

Für mich kommt eine der besten Definitionen von Oper aus einer ziemlich unwahrscheinlichen Quelle: Lee Strasberg beschreibt Oper „nicht als Drama *mit* Musik, sondern Drama *in der* Musik". Deborah Voigts Künstlertum besteht eben darin. [...] Niemals lügt sie auf der Bühne. Denn sie offenbart eine große Portion ihrer selbst auf der Bühne, wie es nur die größten Schauspieler tun können. «

Jack Doulin
Auszug aus seiner Laudatio auf Deborah Voigt

» Herzlichen Glückwunsch, Deborah, zum Piscator Preis. [...] Alexandra Kauka, die heute den Piscator Ehrenpreis erhält, hat unsere Bravorufe ebenso verdient. Alexandra ist eine weniger besungene Heldin der Met, aber eine, ohne die wir nicht florieren könnten. Durch ihr passioniertes Mäzenatentum der Met hilft sie, unsere Kunstform zu retten.

[...]
Sie ist aber auch selbst ein Star. Das stellte ich letzten Sommer fest, als ich mich mit ihr bei den Salzburger Festspielen verabredet hatte. Während ich vor dem Festspielhaus auf sie wartete – gespannt auf die Figaro-Vorstellung mit Anna Netrebko, eine von Alexandras Freundinnen und Lieblingskünstlerinnen – bemerkte ich einen Ansturm von Paparazzi vor dem Theater. Ich vermutete, dass sie auf die Ankunft von Netrebko warteten. In Wahrheit erwarteten sie das Eintreffen von Alexandra. «

Peter Gelb
Auszug aus seiner Laudatio auf Alexandra Kauka

» Liebe Marta Eggerth, was macht Sie so besonders? [...] Wie Maria Callas in der Oper, ist niemand auf dem Gebiet der Operette so weit gegangen wie Sie. Wenn Sie Operetten singen, werden Ihre Rollen nicht nur lebendig, sie werden überlebensgroß!
[...] Oper tendiert zum Tragischen und kann mit Rotwein verglichen werden. Operette ist eher wie Champagner – in vieler Hinsicht sprühend [...] Man glaubt, den Unterschied zu kennen, aber man kennt ihn nicht, bis man nicht Marta Eggerth gehört hat. Mit ihr bekommt der Champagner plötzlich ein Herz, ein Herz voller Gefühl, und meist eine Menge Sex Appeal.
[...] Liebe Marta Eggerth, selbst wenn Sie einen Preis fürs Lebenswerk erhalten, heißt das nicht, dass Sie ausruhen können [...] Wir alle ermutigen Sie: Geben Sie Ihr Geheimnis an die jungen Generationen weiter! Hören Sie nicht das Flehen von Lehár, Kálmán und vielen anderen, die Sie leidenschaftlich verehren? «

Dr. Christoph Thun-Hohenstein
Auszug aus seiner Laudatio auf Marta Eggerth

2008

Edward Albee

Piscator Award, Leading American Playwright, born 1928
Piscator Preis, Führender Amerikanischer Dramatiker, geboren 1928

Edward Albee is considered the most important living American playwright. He burst onto the theatrical scene in the late 1950s with a variety of plays detailing the agonies and disillusionment of that decade. His works include *Who's Afraid of Virginia Woolf?*, *The Zoo Story*, *The Sandbox*, *Three Tall Women*, *Seascape*, *The American Dream*, *The Goat or Who is Sylvia?*, and *Me, Myself and I*. He has received three Pulitzer Prizes for Drama, a Special Tony Award for Lifetime Achievement and the National Medal of Arts.

Albee describes his body of work as "an examination of the American Scene, an attack on the substitution of artificial for real values in our society, a condemnation of complacency, cruelty, and emasculation and vacuity, a stand against the fiction that everything in this slipping land of ours is peachy-keen."

Albee tirelessly promotes American university theater and frequently speaks at campuses. He is the President of the Edward F. Albee Foundation, which maintains a writers and artists colony in Montauk, New York.

Edward Albee gilt als der bedeutendste lebende amerikanische Dramatiker. In den späten 1950er Jahren eroberte er die Theaterszene mit einer Vielzahl von Stücken, welche die Desillusionierung und Agonie dieser Dekade im Einzelnen analysierten. Zu seinen Bühnenwerken gehören *Wer hat Angst vor Virginia Woolf?*, *Die Zoogeschichte*, *Der Sandkasten*, *Drei große Frauen*, *Strandläufer*, *Der amerikanische Traum*, *Die Ziege oder Wer ist Sylvia?*, und *Me, Myself and I*. Er gewann drei Pulitzer Preise für Drama, einen Tony fürs Lebenswerk und die nationale Kunstmedaille.

Albee beschreibt sein Werk als „Untersuchung des amerikanischen Alltags, als Angriff auf das Ersetzen echter Werte in unserer Gesellschaft durch künstliche, als Verurteilung von Selbstgefälligkeit, Grausamkeit, und Geistlosigkeit, ein Statement gegen die Fiktion, dass alles in diesem uns entgleitenden Land toll ist."

Albee wirbt unermüdlich für das universitäre Theater in Amerika und spricht regelmäßig in Hochschulen. Er ist Präsident der Edward F. Albee Stiftung, die eine Künstlerkolonie in Montauk unterhält.

Meera T. Gandhi

Honorary Piscator Award, Indian Businesswoman and Humanitarian, born 1963
Piscator Ehrenpreis, Indische Geschäftsfrau und Philanthropin, geboren 1963

Since high school, Meera T. Gandhi has worked closely with Mother Teresa's Asha Dan home and has been associated with The Happy Home and School for the Blind in Mumbai since 1997, when she also founded the International Playschool of Mumbai. She has been a trustee of the board of I-Create, a non profit organization that creates jobs for women in 22 Indian villages.

In 2000, she purchased and oversaw the renovation of an historical New York City landmark, the former home of First Lady Eleanor Roosevelt.

She is the founder and CEO of The Giving Back Foundation, a foundation geared towards alleviating illness, poverty and suffering while also addressing education issues which affect women and children around the world. She is particularly interested in education as the stepping stone to success.

Married to Vikram Gandhi and the mother of three children, Meera's life motto is: "We are to the universe only as much as we give to it."

Seit der Oberschule arbeitet Meera T. Gandhi eng zusammen mit Mutter Teresas Asha Dan Haus. Seit 1997 ist sie auch mit The Happy Home and School for the Blind in Mumbai verbunden, wo sie im selben Jahr ihre eigenen Internationalen Kindergarten gründete. Als Trustee engagiert sie sich bei der gemeinnützigen Organisation I-Create, die in 22 indischen Dörfern Arbeitsplätze für Frauen schafft.

Im Jahr 2000 kaufte sie das denkmalgeschützte frühere Haus von Eleanor Roosevelt in Manhattan und renovierte es von Grund auf.

Meera Gandhi ist Gründerin und Vorsitzende der Giving Back Foundation. Ihre Stiftung will Krankheit, Armut und Leid lindern, widmet sich gleichzeitig aber auch der Erziehung und Bildung von Frauen und Kindern auf der ganzen Welt, da Erziehung ein Sprungbrett zum Erfolg ist.

Meera und ihr Mann Vikram Gandhi haben drei Kinder. Meeras Leitspruch lautet: „Unsere Bedeutung für das Universum besteht nur in dem Grad, in dem wir etwas zu demselben beitragen."

1 Robert LuPone (left), then Director of the Drama Program at the New School, and the South-African actor Brian Murray

2 Joyce B. Ayoub (right) talks with Andreas Stadler, Director of the Austrian Cultural Forum New York, at the reception prior to the Piscator Award on February 26, 2008 in the library of the Lotos Club

3 Actress Marian Seldes (left), who introduced Edward Albee, with Evelyn Kupin

4 Mary Ann and Dr. Klaus Böhlhoff with Ruth A. Mueller, and Jolana Blau (from right)

5 Edward Albee (center), the Piscator Award recipient of 2008, with Marian Seldes (left), who acted in many original productions of Albee's plays, and Dr. Brigitta Blaha

1 Robert LuPone (links), damals noch Leiter des Drama Programms der New School, und der südafrikanische Schauspieler Brian Murray

2 Joyce B. Ayoub (rechts) unterhält sich am 26. Februar 2008 beim Empfang in der Bibliothek des Lotos Clubs mit dem Direktor des Österreichischen Kulturforums New York Andreas Stadler

3 Die Schauspielerin Marian Seldes (links), welche die Laudatio auf Edward Albee hielt, mit Evelyn Kupin

4 Mary Ann und Dr. Klaus Böhlhoff mit Ruth A. Mueller und Jolana Blau (v.r.n.l.)

5 Der Piscator Preisträger 2008 Edward Albee (Mitte) mit Marian Seldes (links), die als Schauspielerin in zahlreichen seiner Stücke mitwirkte, und Dr. Brigitta Blaha

6 Meera T. Gandhi (center), Honorary Piscator Award Recipient of 2008, with her friends Lucia Hwong Gordon (right), and Jaswant Lalwani

7 Kerry Kennedy (right), President of the Robert F. Kennedy Center for Justice & Human Rights and advisor of The Lahr von Leïtis Academy & Archive, with Michael Lahr (left), and Gregorij von Leïtis

8 Susan Kohner Weitz (left) talks with Hubertus Prince of Sachsen-Coburg-Gotha

9 Anna-Maria Kellen, and Sterling Morton Hamill (both sitting in the foreground), as well as Gregorij von Leïtis (standing) listen to the remarks of Louise Kerz Hirschfeld

10 Dr. Monika Kalista (2nd from left), who is in charge of culture and sport in the state of Salzburg, came specifically from Austria to the Piscator Award. Before flying back to Europe she enjoys a moment with Jan and Jana Storbeck (right), and Michael Lahr

6 Meera T. Gandhi (Mitte), Piscator Ehrenpreisträgerin 2008, mit ihren Freunden Lucia Hwong Gordon (rechts) und Jaswant Lalwani

7 Kerry Kennedy (rechts), Präsidentin des Robert F. Kennedy Center for Justice & Human Rights und Beiratsmitglied von The Lahr von Leïtis Academy & Archive, mit Michael Lahr (links) und Gregorij von Leïtis

8 Susan Kohner Weitz (links) unterhält sich mit Hubertus Prinz von Sachsen-Coburg-Gotha

9 Anna-Maria Kellen und Sterling Morton Hamill (beide sitzend im Vordergrund) und Gregorij von Leïtis (stehend) lauschen den Ausführungen von Louise Kerz Hirschfeld

10 Hofrätin Dr. Monika Kalista (2.v.l.), die im Land Salzburg für Kultur und Sport zuständig ist, war eigens aus Österreich zur Piscator Preisverleihung angereist. Vor dem Rückflug genießt sie einen Moment des Gesprächs mit Jan und Jana Storbeck (rechts) und Michael Lahr

2009

Marian Seldes

Piscator Award, American Actress and Teacher, born 1928
Piscator Preis, Amerikanische Schauspielerin und Lehrerin, geboren 1928

Marian Seldes, a native New Yorker, is a stage, film, radio and television actress whose career has spanned six decades. In 1996 she was elected to the Theater Hall of Fame. She studied acting at the Neighborhood Playhouse and made her Broadway debut in 1957 with Judith Anderson in *Medea*.
Marian Seldes earned four Tony nominations, winning in 1967 for her performance in Edward Albee's *A Delicate Balance*.

In addition to live theater, Marian Seldes began acting in television in 1952. She also performed in a number of motion pictures and radio plays. Among her more recent film credits are *August Rush*, *The Visitor*, *Leatherheads*, and *The Extra Man*.

Marian Seldes appeared in every one of the 1809 Broadway performances of Ira Levin's play *Deathtrap* – a feat that earned her a mention in the *Guinness Book of World Records* as "most durable actress."

From 1967 to 1991, she was a faculty member of the Juilliard School of Drama, and from 2002 to 2005 she taught at Fordham University.

Die gebürtige New Yorkerin Marian Seldes ist eine Bühnen-, Film-, Radio- und Fernsehschauspielerin und seit sechs Jahrzehnten aktiv. 1996 wurde sie in die Theater Hall of Fame aufgenommen. Ausgebildet am Neighborhood Playhouse hatte sie ihr Broadway-Debüt 1957 mit Judith Anderson in *Medea*.
Marian Seldes wurde viermal für den Tony Preis nominiert und gewann ihn 1967 für ihre Rolle in Albees *Empfindliches Gleichgewicht*.

Neben dem Theater übernahm Marian Seldes ab 1952 auch Fernsehrollen und spielte in einer Reihe von Kinofilmen und Hörspielen. Zu ihren jüngsten Filmen gehören *Der Klang des Herzens*, *Ein Sommer in New York*, *Ein verlockendes Spiel* und *Der letzte Gentleman*.

Marian Seldes stand in jeder einzelnen der 1.809 Broadway-Aufführungen von Ira Levins *Das Mörderspiel* auf der Bühne. Diese Tatsache brachte ihr einen Eintrag ins *Guinness Buch der Rekorde* als „beständigste Schauspielerin".

Von 1967 bis 1991 war sie Mitglied des Lehrkörpers der Juilliard School of Drama, von 2002 bis 2005 unterrichtete sie an der Fordham University.

Lya Friedrich Pfeifer

Honorary Piscator Award, American President of the Max Kade Foundation, Inc.
Piscator Ehrenpreis, Amerikanische Präsidentin der Max Kade Foundation, Inc.

Lya Friedrich Pfeifer has been serving as President of the Max Kade Foundation since 2004.

The Max Kade Foundation was established in New York in 1944 by Max Kade, a German-born businessman, who came to the US and founded a successful pharmaceutical company. The foundation's principal interest is in higher education and academic research at a postdoctoral level. The second major interest of the Max Kade Foundation is in improving international understanding and promoting cultural exchanges by supporting the study of German language and culture at American colleges and universities.

Lya Friedrich Pfeifer studied German literature and philosophy at Syracuse University and Law at Touro College. In addition to her position as President of the Max Kade Foundation, she is Director of the German-American School Association, Director of the German-American Partnership Program, Director of the German Society of the City of New York, Vice President of the Liederkranz, and Trustee of the Liederkranz Foundation New York.

Lya Friedrich Pfeifer ist seit 2004 Präsidentin der Max Kade Foundation.

Die Max Kade Foundation wurde 1944 in New York von dem deutschstämmigen Geschäftsmann Max Kade gegründet, der nach Amerika auswanderte und dort eine erfolgreiche Pharma-Firma gründete. Hauptzweck der Stiftung ist die Hochschulbildung und wissenschaftliche Forschung für Post-Doktoranden. Zweites Augenmerk der Stiftung liegt auf der Verbesserung der internationalen Verständigung und der Förderung des kulturellen Austauschs durch die zielgerichtete Unterstützung des Studiums der deutschen Sprache und Kultur an amerikanischen Unis.

Lya Friedrich Pfeifer studierte Germanistik und Philosophie an der Universität in Syracuse und Jura am Touro College. Außer ihrer Position als Präsidentin der Max Kade Foundation ist sie Direktorin der Deutsch-Amerikanischen Schulvereinigung, des Deutsch-Amerikanischen Partnerschaftsprogramms und der Deutschen Gesellschaft der Stadt New York, sowie Vizepräsidentin des Liederkranzes und Trustee der Liederkranz Stiftung in New York.

1 Lya Friedrich Pfeifer (left), and Gregorij von Leïtis expect the arrival of the guests on March 3, 2009 at the Lotos Club

2 Lila Teich Gold regularly attends the Piscator Award Luncheons

3 Dr. Horst Freitag (left), the German Consul General in New York, welcomes the honorees of the year 2009, Lya Friedrich Pfeifer (center), and Marian Seldes

4 Freya Jeschke, who has been volunteering for Elysium for many years, Hubertus Prince of Sachsen-Coburg-Gotha, Alexandra Kauka, and tenor Gabriel Gargari, who sang during the Award Ceremony (from left)

5 Two loyal guests of the Piscator Awards: Jolana Blau (right), Vice President of the Board of Directors of Elysium, and Dr. Robert J. Campbell, author of the authoritative *Campbell's Psychiatric Dictionary*

1 Lya Friedrich Pfeifer (links) und Gregorij von Leïtis erwarten am 3. März 2009 die Ankunft der Gäste im Lotos Club

2 Lila Teich Gold kommt seit Jahren regelmäßig zur Piscator Preisverleihung

3 Dr. Horst Freitag (links), der deutsche Generalkonsul in New York, begrüßt die beiden Preisträgerinnen des Jahres 2009 Lya Friedrich Pfeifer (Mitte) und Marian Seldes

4 Freya Jeschke, die seit vielen Jahren ehrenamtlich für Elysium tätig ist, Hubertus Prinz von Sachsen-Coburg-Gotha, Alexandra Kauka und der Tenor Gabriel Gargari, der die Preisverleihung musikalisch umrahmte (v.l.n.r.)

5 Zwei treue Gäste der Piscator Preisverleihungen: Jolana Blau (rechts), stellvertretende Vorsitzende des Vorstandes von Elysium, und Dr. Robert J. Campbell, Autor des Standardwerkes *Campbell's Psychiatric Dictionary*

6 Carol G. Walter (left), and Dr. Horst Freitag

7 Lively conversations around the table: Jolana Blau, Dr. Horst Freitag, Ingrid Lindstrom Leitzen, Wolfgang Doerr, and Monika Abbott (from left)

8 Christa von Hassell (left), art historian and widow of the former German UN-Ambassador Wolf Ulrich von Hassell, with Michael Lahr

9 After the Award Ceremony this spontaneous group photo was taken: Lya Friedrich Pfeifer, Marian Seldes, Susan Kohner Weitz, Judith Malina, Gregorij von Leïtis, Dr. Brigitta Blaha, Daniel Hoster, who introduced Lya Friedrich Pfeifer, and Joseph R. Pfeifer, President of the Liederkranz Foundation (from left)

6 Carol G. Walter (links) und Dr. Horst Freitag

7 Lebhafte Gespräche rund um den Tisch: Jolana Blau, Dr. Horst Freitag, Ingrid Lindstrom Leitzen, Wolfgang Doerr und Monika Abbott (v.l.n.r.)

8 Christa von Hassell (links), Kunsthistorikerin und Witwe des früheren deutschen UN-Botschafters Wolf Ulrich von Hassell, mit Michael Lahr

9 Nach dem Festakt entsteht dieses spontane Gruppenbild: Lya Friedrich Pfeifer, Marian Seldes, Susan Kohner Weitz, Judith Malina, Gregorij von Leïtis, Dr. Brigitta Blaha, Daniel Hoster, der die Ehrenrede auf Lya Friedrich Pfeifer gehalten hat, und Joseph R. Pfeifer, Präsident der Liederkranz Foundation (v.l.n.r.)

2010

Martina Arroyo

Piscator Award, American Soprano and Teacher, born 1937
Piscator Preis, Amerikanische Sopranistin und Lehrerin, geboren 1937

Martina Arroyo was part of the first generation of black opera singers to achieve wide success. She first rose to prominence at the Zurich opera in 1963. From 1965 to 1978 she was one of the leading sopranos at the Metropolitan Opera. She was famous for her interpretations of Verdi, Puccini, Strauss, and Mozart. Equally at ease with contemporary music, she sang the world premiere of Samuel Barber's *Andromache's Farewell* and Karlheinz Stockhausen's *Momente*. Arroyo made more than 50 recordings of major operas and orchestral works.

Appointed by President Gerald Ford, she served on the board of the National Endowment for the Arts for six years. In addition, she is associated with the National Council on the Arts as an Ambassador for the Arts.

She has taught at various universities, including the School of Music of Indiana University. In 2003, she established The Martina Arroyo Foundation, offering the study and preparation of complete operatic roles to emerging young artists.

Martina Arroyo gehört der ersten Generation schwarzer Opernsänger an, denen der Durchbruch auf die großen Opernbühnen gelang. In Zürich begann 1963 ihre Laufbahn. Von 1965 bis 1978 war sie eine der führenden Soprane der Metropolitan Opera und berühmt für ihre Interpretationen von Verdi, Puccini, Strauss und Mozart. Das zeitgenössische Repertoire lag ihr ebenso: sie sang die Welturaufführung von Samuel Barbers *Andromache's Farewell* und Karlheinz Stockhausens *Momente*. Arroyo spielte Aufnahmen bedeutender Opern und Orchesterwerke ein.

Präsident Gerald Ford berief sie ins National Endowment for the Arts (NEA), eine Stiftung der USA zur Förderung von Kunst und Kultur. Als Botschafterin der Künste ist sie dem NEA bis heute beratend verbunden.

Arroyo hat an diversen Universitäten unterrichtet, u.a. am Musikkonservatorium der Universität Indiana. Mit ihrer 2003 gegründeten Martina Arroyo Stiftung bietet sie angehenden jungen Künstlern das strukturierte Studium und die Vorbereitung kompletter Opernrollen an.

Carol Kahn Strauss

Honorary Piscator Award, American Custodian of the German-Jewish Legacy
Piscator Ehrenpreis, Amerikanische Bewahrerin des Deutsch-Jüdischen Erbes

For 18 years, Carol Kahn Strauss served as Executive Director of the Leo Baeck Institute in New York. In 2012 she became the Institute's International Director, maintaining and deepening the Leo Baeck Institute's relationships with partners abroad.

The Leo Baeck Institute (LBI) is a research library and archive that documents the history and culture of German-speaking Jewry, primarily in the 19th and 20th century, but includes documents dating back to the middle ages. It was founded in 1955 as a repository for the documents that could be salvaged from a decimated Central Europe. Without the Leo Baeck Institute many of these priceless treasures would have been lost to history.

Under Carol Kahn Strauss's leadership as Executive Director, the Institute massively expanded its collections and capacity. She also intensified the Institute's ties to the Federal Republic of Germany and was instrumental in the establishment of the Berlin Branch of LBI's Archives.

In 2005, she was honored with the Order of Merit, The Cross of Merit, First Class, of the Federal Republic of Germany.

18 Jahre lang war Carol Kahn Strauss Geschäftsführerin des Leo Baeck Instituts in New York. Seit 2012 ist sie als Internationale Direktorin des Instituts zuständig für die Kontakt- und Beziehungspflege zu den ausländischen Partnern.

Das Leo Baeck Institut (LBI) ist Forschungsbibliothek und Archiv für die Geschichte und Kultur des deutschsprachigen Judentums. Schwerpunkt der Sammlung ist das 19. und 20. Jahrhundert, doch es gibt auch Dokumente aus dem Mittelalter. Es wurde 1955 gegründet, um die Bücher, Papiere und Photos eines durch den Holocaust extrem reduzierten mitteleuropäischen Judentums zu retten. Ohne das LBI wären viele dieser Schätze für immer verloren gegangen.

Unter Carol Kahn Strauss' Leitung expandierte das Institut seine Sammlung massiv. Carol Kahn Strauss intensivierte auch die Beziehungen nach Deutschland und half, eine Niederlassung des Archivs im Jüdischen Museum Berlin zu etablieren.

2005 wurde Carol Kahn Strauss das Bundesverdienstkreuz erster Klasse verliehen.

Luise Rainer

Piscator Lifetime Achievement Award, German-Born Actress, born 1910
Piscator Preis fürs Lebenswerk, Deutschstämmige Schauspielerin, geboren 1910

Luise Rainer was the first woman to win two Academy Awards. She won her two Oscars for Best Actress in two consecutive years. Born in Düsseldorf, Germany, she started her acting training at age 16 with Max Reinhardt. Talent scouts of Metro-Goldwyn-Mayer discovered her and brought her to Hollywood in 1935. In 1936 she played a relatively small part in *The Great Ziegfeld*, but her presence on the screen so impressed audiences that she won her first Oscar. A year later she portrayed a poor uncomely Chinese farm wife in the film adaptation of Pearl S. Buck's novel *The Good Earth*, winning her another Academy Award.

In 1938 she abandoned the film industry and soon thereafter moved to New York to live with her first husband, the playwright Clifford Odets. In 1940, she played the title role in George Bernard Shaw's *Saint John* directed by Erwin Piscator at the Belasco Theatre in Washington, D.C. With her second husband, Robert Knittel, Luise Rainer moved to London.

Sporadically she has made television and stage appearances after her move to England.

Luise Rainer war die erste Frau, die zwei Oscars gewann, und dies in zwei aufeinanderfolgenden Jahren. Geboren in Düsseldorf, nahm sie schon mit 16 Jahren Schauspielunterricht bei Max Reinhardt. Talentsucher von Metro-Goldwyn-Mayer entdeckten sie und brachten sie 1935 nach Hollywood. 1936 spielte sie eine relativ kleine Rolle in *Der große Ziegfeld*, doch ihre Präsenz beeindruckte das Publikum so sehr, dass sie ihren ersten Oscar gewann. Ein Jahr später verkörperte sie eine arme unattraktive chinesische Bäuerin in der Verfilmung von Pearl S. Bucks Roman *Die gute Erde*, und wurde dafür mit dem zweiten Oscar ausgezeichnet.

1938 kehrte sie der Filmindustrie den Rücken und zog wenig später zu ihrem ersten Mann, dem Dramatiker Clifford Odets, nach New York. 1940 spielte sie die Titelrolle in George Bernard Shaws *Die heilige Johanna*, ein Stück, das Erwin Piscator am Belasco Theater in Washington, D.C. inszenierte.

Mit ihrem zweiten Mann Robert Knittel ließ sie sich später in London nieder und hatte dort immer wieder vereinzelte Fernseh- und Bühnenauftritte.

Christine Ostermayer

Piscator Jubilee Award, Austrian Actress, born 1936
Piscator Jubiläumspreis, Österreichische Schauspielerin, geboren 1936

Christine Ostermayer was part of the ensemble of the Residenz Theater in Munich for 20 years. She had her debut as Minni Fay in Thornton Wilder's *The Matchmaker* at the Theater Essen. Further stops were the Wuppertal City Theater, the Schauspielhaus and the Kammerspiele Hamburg, Berlin's Schiller Theater, Vienna's Burgtheater, Munich's Volkstheater, and Vienna's Theater in der Josefstadt, where she was engaged from 1988 to 1993.

At the Salzburg Festival, she played Salome in Nestroy's *Der Talisman*, and played various roles in the *Jedermann* peformances there. She was seen on TV in various literature films, for instance in *Countess Mizzi* based on Arthur Schnitzler.

She was honored with the Kainz Medal of the Burgtheater and the Nestroy Ring of Vienna.
For her role as Rosa suffering from cancer in the film *Anfang 80*, she received the prize as best actress at the Film Festival Graz, Austria. In the film *Nebenwege* (2012), she plays the role of a woman ill with dementia, who disappears as her son wants to take her to a nursing home.

Christine Ostermayer zählte 20 Jahre lang zum Ensemble des Münchner Residenztheaters. Ihr Debüt hatte sie als Minni Fay in Thornton Wilders *Heiratsvermittlerin* am Theater Essen. Weitere Stationen waren die Städtischen Bühnen Wuppertal, das Schauspielhaus und die Kammerspiele Hamburg, das Berliner Schillertheater, das Wiener Burghtheater, das Volkstheater München und das Theater in der Josefstadt in Wien, wo sie von 1988 bis 1993 engagiert war.

Bei den Salzburger Festspielen verkörperte sie die Salome in Nestroys *Der Talisman* und wirkte mehrfach in verschiedenen Rollen bei den dortigen *Jedermann*-Aufführungen mit.
Im Fernsehen war sie in diversen Literaturverfilmungen zu sehen, etwa in *Komtesse Mizzi* nach Arthur Schnitzler.

Sie wurde mit der Kainz-Medaille des Burgtheaters und dem Nestroy-Ring der Stadt Wien geehrt.
Für ihre Rolle als krebskranke Rosa im Film *Anfang 80* erhielt sie 2012 den Preis als beste Schauspielerin beim Grazer Filmfestival. Im Film *Nebenwege* (2012) spielt sie eine demenzkranke Frau, die verschwindet, als ihr Sohn sie in ein Pflegeheim bringen will.

1 Honoree Martina Arroyo (left), and speaker Nimet Habachy at the beginning of the 23rd Piscator Award Luncheon on March 2, 2010

2 Soprano Martina Arroyo (left), her husband Michel Maurel (center), and Lya Friedrich Pfeifer, President of the Max Kade Foundation

3 Carol Kahn Strauss (right), who for many years served as Executive Director of the Leo Baeck Institut New York, her husband Peter Strauss (center), and Andreas Stadler

4 Maxi, the dachshund of Elke and Ben Gazzara, and the cover of Elke Gazzara's dog biography Madison Avenue Maxi

5 Art historian Dr. Philipp Gutbrod (right), who is now curator of the Institute Mathildenhöhe in Darmstadt / Germany, with Gregorij von Leïtis

1 Preisträgerin Martina Arroyo (links) und ihre Laudatorin Nimet Habachy vor der 23. Piscator Preisverleihung am 2. März 2010

2 Sopran Martina Arroyo (links), ihr Mann Michel Maurel (Mitte) und Lya Friedrich Pfeifer, Präsidentin der Max Kade Foundation

3 Carol Kahn Strauss (rechts), langjährige Geschäftsführerin des Leo Baeck Instituts New York, ihr Mann Peter Strauss (Mitte) und Andreas Stadler

4 Maxi, der Dackel von Elke und Ben Gazzara, und das von Elke Gazzara über ihn geschriebene Buch Madison Avenue Maxi

5 Der Kunsthistoriker Dr. Philipp Gutbrod (rechts), heute Kurator am Institut Mathildenhöhe in Darmstadt, mit Gregorij von Leïtis

6 Dr. Martin Bussmann (2nd from right), who has been supporting the work of Elysium for many years, with his guests (from left): Ted Nardin, Andrea Berkowitz, and Karen Furey of the American Council on Germany

7 Anneliese Langner (seating at left), founder of the Dimicare Anneliese Langner Foundation, with Elysium's devoted US-board member Jolana Blau (seating at right), as well as Ingrid Lindstrom Leitzen, Daniel and Joy Ferro (standing from left)

8 Dan Franklin Smith, the Music Director of Elysium – between two continents

9 Gregorij von Leïtis (left), meets with Luise Rainer, who received the Erwin Piscator Lifetime Achievement Award 2010, a few weeks after the Award Ceremony in Ms. Rainer's apartment in London

6 Dr. Martin Bussmann (2.v.r.), der seit Jahren die Arbeit von Elysium unterstützt, mit seinen Gästen (v.l.n.r.): Ted Nardin, Andrea Berkowitz und Karen Furey vom American Council on Germany

7 Anneliese Langner (sitzend links), Gründerin der Dimicare Anneliese Langner Stiftung, mit Elysiums langjährigem US-Vorstandsmitglied Jolana Blau (sitzend rechts), sowie Ingrid Lindstrom Leitzen, Daniel und Joy Ferro (stehend v.l.n.r.)

8 Dan Franklin Smith, viele Jahre lang der Musikdirektor von Elysium – between two continents

9 Gregorij von Leïtis (links) trifft die Trägerin des Erwin Piscator Lifetime Achievement Award 2010 Luise Rainer einige Wochen nach der Preisverleihung in ihrer Londoner Wohnung

1 In celebration of the 25th anniversary of the Founding of the Erwin Piscator Award, a Jubilee Award was presented on December 16, 2010, one day before Erwin Piscator's birthday. Among the many guests at the Ceremony at the Künstlerhaus in Munich were (in the first row from left): Dr. Thomas Goppel, Jubilee Award Recipient Christine Ostermayer, Gregorij von Leïtis, Rose Marie Countess Königsdorff, Dr. Bernd-A. von Maltzan, and Karin von Bülow

2 Dr. Thomas Goppel (standing), the former Bavarian State Minister for Science, Research and the Arts, spoke about Christine Ostermayer

3 Dr. Thomas Goppel, Maja Grassinger, President of the Künstlerhaus in Munich, and Michael Lahr toast Christine Ostermayer after the Award Ceremony (from right)

4 Dr. Michael Dietl (left) in conversation with Dr. Bernd-A. von Maltzan

1 Anläßlich des 25jährigen Gründungsjubiläums des Erwin Piscator Preises wird am 16. Dezember 2010, einen Tag vor Piscators Geburtstag, einmalig der Piscator Jubiläumspreis vergeben. Unter den zahlreichen Gästen im Künstlerhaus München sind (in der 1. Reihe v.l.n.r.): Dr. Thomas Goppel, die Jubiläumspreisträgerin Christine Ostermayer, Gregorij von Leïtis, Rose Marie Gräfin von Königsdorff, Dr. Bernd-A. von Maltzan und Karin von Bülow

2 Dr. Thomas Goppel (stehend), der ehemalige Bayerische Staatsminister für Wissenschaft, Forschung und Kunst, hält die Laudatio auf Christine Ostermayer

3 Dr. Thomas Goppel, Maja Grassinger, die Präsidentin des Münchner Künstlerhauses, und Michael Lahr stoßen mit Christine Ostermayer nach dem Festakt an (v.r.n.l.)

4 Dr. Michael Dietl (links) im Gespräch mit Dr. Bernd-A. von Maltzan

» I think one of the best stories of all is the day there was a very particular call from Mr. Bing requesting that Martina go on that very night as Aida for an ailing Birgit Nilsson. As many of Martina's friends had taken to imitating Mr. Bing, Martina assumed it was a prank. So she replied that as it was Saturday, she would be taking her mother to the movies, but since the movies ended towards 5 in the afternoon, yes, she would be able to come down and sing at the Met. Wouldn't you have loved to be with Martina when she realized this was the real thing? And Martina's debut was a smashing success! [...]
The love and support Martina has received, she now gives, not only to friends, but to the kids who partake of her extraordinary summer program. «

Nimet Habachy
Excerpts from her remarks on Martina Arroyo

» Let's toast to a tremendous personality who turned the Leo Baeck Institute into the heart and soul of preserving the past of German-speaking Jewry who emigrated to the United States. She is the nucleus of an eminently important organization in building a transatlantic bridge from past personal experience to collective memory and one who continues to deserve our full and wholehearted support.
[...] Simply put, Carol's work proves that the history of Jews in Germany is in point of fact the history of Germans. This is a message that Carol has championed: that "Jewish life" is not a marginal or distant segment of German society. Rather, it has formed a crucial part of German life and contributed in such great measure to German Enlightenment, to democracy and to liberal society in modern Germany. [...] Carol is [...] a vivid example that Jewish life has again become an integral part of our society in Germany. «

Dr. Horst Freitag
Excerpts from his remarks on Carol Kahn Strauss

» Eine der besten Geschichten ist die von jenem Anruf, als Rudolf Bing Martina bat, am selben Abend für die kranke Birgit Nilsson als Aida einzuspringen. Viele Freunde von Martina hatten sich angewöhnt, die Stimme von Herrn Bing nachzuahmen, und so dachte Martina, dies sei ein Streich. Sie antwortete, dass heute Samstag sei und sie ihre Mutter ins Kino ausführen würde, da das Kino aber gegen 5.00 Uhr nachmittags beendet sei, könne sie durchaus danach kommen und in der Met singen. Wären nicht auch Sie gerne dabei gewesen, als Martina feststellte, dass der echte Rudolf Bing am Apparat war? Martinas Debüt war ein Riesenerfolg! [...]
Die Zuneigung und Unterstützung, die Martina erfahren hat, gibt sie nun zurück, nicht nur an ihre Freunde, sondern an junge Menschen, die an ihrem außergewöhnlichen Sommerprogramm teilnehmen. «

Nimet Habachy
Auszug aus ihrer Laudatio auf Martina Arroyo

» Lassen Sie uns anstoßen auf eine tolle Persönlichkeit, die das Leo Baeck Institut zum wahren Zentrum für die Bewahrung des deutschsprachigen Judentums in der US-Emigration gemacht hat. Sie ist der Kern einer Organisation, die für den transatlantischen Brückenbau besonders wichtig ist, von der vergangenen persönlichen Erfahrung hin zum kollektiven Gedächtnis. Und sie verdient weiterhin unsere volle rückhaltlose Unterstützung.
[...] Einfach ausgedrückt: Carols Arbeit zeigt, dass die Geschichte der Juden in Deutschland in Wirklichkeit die Geschichte der Deutschen ist. Carols Botschaft lautet: Jüdisches Leben ist nicht eine Randerscheinung oder ein entferntes Teilstück der deutschen Gesellschaft. Es hat vielmehr einen entscheidenden Teil des deutschen Lebens geprägt und hat maßgeblich zur deutschen Aufklärung, zur Demokratie und einer liberalen Gesellschaft in Deutschland beigetragen. [...] Carol ist [...] ein lebendes Beispiel dafür, dass jüdisches Leben erneut integraler Bestandteil unserer Gesellschaft in Deutschland geworden ist. «

Dr. Horst Freitag
Auszug aus seiner Laudatio auf Carol Kahn Strauss

2011

E. L. Doctorow

Piscator Award, American Writer and Professor, born 1931
Piscator Preis, Amerikanischer Autor und Hochschullehrer, geboren 1931

E. L. Doctorow's work has been published in thirty-two languages. A native of the Bronx, he is internationally known for his unique works of historical fiction.

His novels include *The March*, *City of God*, *Welcome to Hard Times*, *The Book of Daniel*, *Ragtime*, *Loon Lake*, *World's Fair*, *Billy Bathgate*, *The Waterworks*, and *Homer & Langley*. He has published two volumes of short fiction and several collections of essays.

There have been five film adaptations of his work. His book *Ragtime* was named one of the 100 best novels of the 20th century by the Modern Library editorial board. It was adapted for the musical theater and returned to Broadway in 2010 in a highly acclaimed Kennedy Center revival.

He won the National Book Award, the PEN / Saul Bellow Award for Achievement in American Fiction, and the presidentially conferred National Humanities Medal.

E. L. Doctorow has taught at the Yale School of Drama and Princeton University, and currently holds the Lewis and Loretta Glucksman Chair of English and American Letters at New York University.

E. L. Doctorows Werke sind in 32 Sprachen übersetzt. Im New Yorker Stadtteil Bronx geboren, ist er international bekannt für seine einzigartigen historischen Romane, darunter *Der Marsch*, *City of God*, *Willkommen in Hard Times*, *Das Buch Daniel*, *Ragtime*, *Sterntaucher*, *Weltausstellung*, *Billy Bathgate*, *Das Wasserwerk* und *Homer & Langley*.

Er hat zwei Bände mit Kurzgeschichten veröffentlicht und drei Essay-Sammlungen.

Fünf seiner Bücher wurden verfilmt. *Ragtime* wurde von den Herausgebern der Modern Library zu einem der 100 besten Romane des 20. Jahrhunderts gezählt. Das Buch diente als Vorlage für ein Musical, welches 2010 in einer Neuinszenierung des Kennedy Center an den Broadway zurückkehrte.

Doctorow hat den National Book Award gewonnen und den PEN / Saul Bellow Award für seine Verdienste um die amerikanische Literatur, außerdem hat ihm Präsident Clinton die National Humanities Medal verliehen. Er hat in Yale und Princeton unterrichtet und ist Lewis und Loretta Glucksman Professor für englische Literatur an der New York University.

Peter Gelb

Honorary Piscator Award, American Arts Administrator and Producer, born 1953
Piscator Ehrenpreis, Amerikanischer Kunstmanager und Produzent, geboren 1953

Peter Gelb's career has followed a singular arc that began with his teenage years as an usher at the Metropolitan Opera and led to his appointment, in 2006, as the storied company's 16th general manager.

Gelb's aim is to revitalize opera and connect it to a wider audience. From the beginning of his tenure at the Met he has recruited the world's great theater directors to enhance the theatricality of the Met's productions. His groundbreaking initiative *The Met: Live in HD*, a series of live performance transmissions in movie theaters, has won an Emmy award. Another priority of his is to bring new productions of classic and modern masterpieces onto the stage.

Prior to his appointment to the helm of the Met, Peter Gelb worked as award-winning producer of films, recordings, concert events and festivals. He collaborated with many of the world's leading artists, including Vladimir Horowitz, Herbert von Karajan, and Luciano Pavarotti. As president of Sony Classical, one of the largest international classical record labels, he led the company through a period of notable growth.

Peter Gelbs beruflicher Werdegang begann, als er im Jugendalter als Platzanweiser in der Metropolitan Opera arbeitete, und mündete 2006 in einem einzigartigen Bogen in seine Berufung zum 16. Generaldirektor dieser geschichtsträchtigen Bühne.

Gelbs erklärtes Ziel ist es, die Oper neu zu beleben und ein größeres Publikum für sie zu gewinnen. Er verpflichtet weltweit führende Theaterregisseure an die Met, um die Theatralität der Opernproduktionen zu steigern. Seine bahnbrechende Initiative *The Met: Live in HD*, eine Serie von Opern-Übertragungen live in Kinos auf der ganzen Welt, gewann den Emmy Preis. Außerdem will er neue Produktionen von klassischen und modernen Meisterwerken inszenieren.

Bevor er Generaldirektor der Met wurde, arbeitete Gelb als preisgekrönter Produzent von Filmen, Tonaufnahmen, Konzerten und Festivals und kooperierte mit vielen Spitzenkünstlern wie Horowitz, Karajan und Pavarotti. Als Präsident von Sony Classical hat er wesentlich zur Expansion dieses großen internationalen klassischen Musiklabels beigetragen.

1 Author and journalist Huberta von Voss-Wittig, Chev. Cesare
L. Santeramo, who served as Chairperson of the Piscator Award
Luncheon Committee from 2011 until 2013, Gregorij von Leïtis,
and the writer Daniel Kehlmann (from left)

2 Judith Malina, Artistic Director of the legendary Living Theatre,
Brad Burgess, and Dr. Helga Rabl-Stadler, President of the
Salzburg Festival (from left)

3 Agnes Jacobs (left) with Jolana Blau at the 24th Piscator Award
Luncheon on March 22, 2011

4 In his remarks Daniel Kehlmann emphasizes how much the
literary œuvre of E. L. Doctorow has shaped him

5 E. L. Doctorow (right) thanks Gregorij von Leïtis and the guests
of the Piscator Award Luncheon 2011 for this recognition

6 Gregorij von Leïtis (left) looks on, while Peter Gelb delivers his
acceptance speech

1 Autorin und Journalistin Huberta von Voss-Wittig, Cesare
L. Santeramo, der von 2011 bis 2013 als Vorsitzender des
Piscator Luncheon Komitees fungierte, Gregorij von Leïtis und der
Schriftsteller Daniel Kehlmann (v.l.n.r.)

2 Judith Malina, Leiterin des legendären Living Theatre, Brad
Burgess und Dr. Helga Rabl-Stadler, Präsidentin der Salzburger
Festspiele (v.l.n.r.)

3 Agnes Jacobs (links) mit Jolana Blau bei der 24. Piscator
Preisverleihung am 22. März 2011

4 Daniel Kehlmann betont in seiner Laudatio auf E.L. Doctorow,
wie sehr dessen literarisches Werk ihn geprägt hat

5 E. L. Doctorow (rechts) bedankt sich für die Auszeichnung bei
Gregorij von Leïtis und den Gästen des Piscator Luncheons 2011

6 Gregorij von Leitis (links) schaut zu, während Peter Gelb seine
Dankesrede hält

» Peter [Gelb] is way up there in the exalted ranks of great impresarios – Belasco, Diaghilev, PT Barnum, Joseph Papp and yes the visionary Piscator whose scale of thinking, brilliant sense of design and refusal to accept boundaries strongly remind me of Peter.
[…]
As far as I can tell, Peter – despite a large and excellent staff – is involved and ultimately responsible for everything that goes on at the Metropolitan Opera. Choosing the repertoire of course, planning with the Music Director, hiring directors and designers, travelling all over the world to see work at other opera houses, dealing with a powerful Board of Directors, raising money, giving speeches, receiving prestigious awards – these are the big public functions. But then there are thousands of little things – reworking press releases, picking the perfect photo for an ad campaign, obsessing about the language of the Met titles, the light on the leading lady, being in all major rehearsals with the director, offering advice, support, suggestions and occasionally cracking a paternal whip.
[…]
A visionary is defined in the dictionary in two ways: as "a person of unusually keen foresight and imagination," or "a person who sees or has visions." Peter fits both definitions and makes them one. I think it is lovely that you are giving an award today named for one of the great theatrical visionaries of the 20th century, to someone who is clearly one of the great theatrical visionaries of the 21st. «

André Bishop
Excerpts from his remarks on Peter Gelb

» Peter [Gelb] ist ganz oben in den erhabenen Rängen großer Impresarios – Belasco, Diaghilev, PT Barnum, Joseph Papp, und der visionäre Piscator, dessen gedankliche Größe, dessen brillantes Gefühl für Design und dessen Weigerung, Grenzen zu akzeptieren, mich sehr stark an Peter erinnern.
[…]
Soweit ich das beurteilen kann, ist Peter – trotz eines großen und hervorragenden Mitarbeiterstabs – einbezogen in und letztlich verantwortlich für alles, was an der Metropolitan Oper geschieht. Die Wahl des Repertoires, die Planung mit dem Musikdirektor, das Engagieren von Regisseuren und Bühnenbildnern, das Reisen um die Welt, um die Aufführungen anderer Opernhäuser zu sehen, der Umgang mit einem mächtigen Vorstand, das Sammeln von Geld, Reden halten, namhafte Preise in Empfang nehmen – dies sind die großen öffentlichen Aufgaben. Darüber hinaus gibt es tausend kleine Dinge – Pressemitteilungen überarbeiten, das richtige Photo für eine Werbekampagne aussuchen, über den Untertiteln brüten, die Hauptdarstellerin ins richtige Licht setzen, in allen großen Proben dabei sein, Ratschläge, Anregungen und Rückhalt geben, und manchmal väterlich ein Machtwort sprechen.
[…]
Ein Visionär wird im Lexikon auf zweifache Weise definiert: als „eine Person von ungewöhnlich scharfer Vorausschau und Vorstellungskraft", oder „als eine Person, die seherische Fähigkeiten hat". Peter erfüllt beide Definitionen und vereint sie in sich. Ich finde es wunderbar, dass Sie heute einen Preis, der nach einem der großen Theatervisionäre des 20. Jahrhunderts benannt ist, verleihen an einen der großen Theatervisionäre des 21. Jahrhunderts. «

André Bishop
Auszug aus seiner Laudatio auf Peter Gelb

» Good art is created by being economical with one's means, but great art needs lavishness, extravagance; it makes it seem as if everything is easy and there are no boundaries to the imagination.

So *Ragtime*: Perhaps the weirdest of all historical novels without which, by the way, I could have never, NEVER, written my novel *Measuring the World, Ragtime*, which plays with American history narrated within the formal means of German romanticism.

[...] Doctorow himself alludes to how much he owes to the style of Heinrich von Kleist and his novella *Michael Kohlhaas*, among other things, with the name of his hero Michael Coalhouse Walker. [...] Kleist was a wild inventor who longed for the strictness of law and objectivity. He wanted his stories, which are full of violence and confusion, to sound like rigorous reports. It is the same tension that drives the unreliable historical work of *Ragtime* where we ask ourselves constantly while reading what is true and what is not until we finally give up and believe everything and nothing. [...]

This thought, that the lives of the departed, their pain and their humiliation, is as relevant to us as those of our contemporaries does have a political side to it. The *Book of Daniel* is literally vibrating with anger about one of the great murders of the American justice system, while *Ragtime* hides no less of an indignation behind its Kleistian cool and there is arguably no other white novelist in Doctorow's generation who confronted the monstrosity of slavery so consciously and emphatically. Many historical figures appear in Doctorow's works but his greatest affections lie with the common people who through cleverness, strength and tenacity need to hold their own against adverse conditions. Naturally, no historian would remember them. Only oblivion awaits them and perhaps the imagination of the novelist who will invent them.
Erwin Piscator was a political activist and avant-gardist at a time when those concepts were not yet termed to be contradictory, an innovator of the stage of such stature that no director has surpassed his radicalness. He was a European who came to America and influenced the artists of this continent, among them Marlon Brando, Lee Strasberg and Tennessee Williams, and who returned to Germany. No other would be a more deserving recipient of this honor than the political avant-gardist E.L.Doctorow who starts every novel again as if it is his first one and who relates America's past in a way that makes us see the America of today as if for the first time. Dear, admired, E.L. Doctorow, I congratulate you on the Erwin-Piscator-prize. «

Daniel Kehlmann
Excerpts from his remarks on E. L. Doctorow

» Gute Literatur entsteht aus Sparsamkeit der Mittel, große aber aus der Verschwendung. Sie erweckt den Anschein, als wäre alles leicht und der Phantasie wären keine Grenzen gesetzt

Ragtime also. Der vielleicht merkwürdigste aller historischen Romane, ohne dessen Vorbild ich - aber das nur ganz nebenbei - niemals meinen Roman *Die Vermessung der Welt* hätte schreiben können. *Ragtime*: ein Spiel mit amerikanischer Geschichte, erzählt mit den formalen Mitteln deutscher Romantik.

[...] Doctorow hat selbst, unter anderem durch den Namen seines Helden Michael Coalhouse Walker darauf hingewiesen, wieviel sein Roman dem Stil Heinrich von Kleists und dessen Novelle *Michael Kohlhaas* verdankt. [...] Kleist war ein wilder Erfinder, der sich nach der Strenge von Gesetz und Sachlichkeit sehnte, er wollte seinen Erzählungen, die voll sind von Gewalt und Verwirrung, den Ton der allerstrengsten Berichte geben. Aus ebendieser Spannung lebt auch das unzuverlässige Geschichtswerk *Ragtime*, bei dessen Lektüre wir uns ständig fragen, was nun eigentlich wahr ist und was erfunden, bis wir endlich die Frage aufgeben und dem Buch alles und nichts mehr glauben. [...]

Der Gedanke, daß die Leben vergangener Generationen, ihre Schmerzen und ihre Erniedrigung, uns so viel angehen wie die unserer Zeitgenossen, hat natürlich eine politische Seite. *Das Buch Daniel* vibriert förmlich vor Zorn über einen der großen Justizmorde der amerikanischen Geschichte, während *Ragtime* eine nicht geringere Empörung hinter der Kleistschen Kühle seiner Prosa verbirgt, und wohl kein weißer Romancier nicht nur in Doctorows Generation hat sich so bewußt dem ungeheuren Skandalon der Sklaverei gestellt. In Doctorows Werk treten viele historische Figuren auf, aber seine größte Zuneigung gilt den einfachen Leuten, die sich mit Schlauheit, Kraft und Zähigkeit gegen widrige Zeitläufte behaupten

müssen. An sie erinnert sich naturgemäß kein Geschichtsschreiber. Auf sie wartet nur das Vergessen und vielleicht die Phantasie eines Romanciers, der ihnen den Dienst tun kann, sie zu erfinden.

Erwin Piscator war politischer Aktivist und Avantgardist zu einem Zeitpunkt, als diese Begriffe noch nicht zum Widerspruch erklärt worden waren, ein Innovator der Bühne von solchem Rang, daß bis heute kein Regisseur ihn an Radikalität übertroffen hat. Seine Arbeit war voll Zorn und zugleich kunstvoll spielerisch, er war ein Europäer, der nach Amerika kam und die Künstler dieses Kontinents prägte, unter anderem Marlon Brando, Lee Strasberg und Tennessee Williams. Es könnte für einen Preis in seinem Namen keinen würdigeren Träger geben als den politischen Avantgardisten E.L. Doctorow, den Historiker und Erfinder, der immer noch jeden Roman beginnt, als wäre es sein erster. «

Daniel Kehlmann
Auszug aus seiner Laudatio auf E. L. Doctorow

Die deutsche Fassung der Laudatio wurde am 7. April 2011 in der Frankfurter Allgemeinen Zeitung abgedruckt unter dem Titel: *Er lernte von Kleist und ich von ihm*

Thomas Hampson

Piscator Award, American Baritone and passionate Educator, born 1955
Piscator Preis, Amerikanischer Bariton und passionierter Lehrer, geboren 1955

Hailing from Spokane, Washington, Thomas Hampson has performed in the world's most important concert halls and opera houses. His operatic repertoire spans a range of more than 80 roles. Commemorating the tenth anniversary of the 9/11 attacks, Thomas Hampson created the role of Rick Rescorla in the world premiere of Christopher Theofanidis's opera *Heart of a Soldier* at San Francisco Opera.

Hampson has won worldwide recognition for his thoughtfully researched and creatively constructed programs that explore the rich repertoire of song in a wide range of styles, languages, and periods. He is one of the most important interpreters of German Romantic song, and with his celebrated *Song of America* project, a collaboration with the Library of Congress, has become the "ambassador" of American Song. Through the Hampsong Foundation, founded in 2003, he employs the art of song to promote intercultural dialogue and understanding.

A passionate teacher, he was recently inducted into the American Academy of Arts and Sciences.

In Spokane, Washington aufgewachsen, ist Thomas Hampson in den großen Opernhäusern und Konzerthallen der Welt aufgetreten. Sein Opernrepertoire umfasst mehr als 80 Rollen. In Erinnerung an den 10. Jahrestag der Terroranschläge vom 11. September sang Thomas Hampson die Rolle des Rick Rescorla in der Welturaufführung von Christopher Theofanidis' *Heart of a Soldier* an der Oper in San Francisco.

Breite Anerkennung genießt Hampson für seine sorgfältig erforschten und außergewöhnlich zusammengestellten Programme, sowie für seine aktive Lehrtätigkeit und die Erkundung des schier unendlichen Liedrepertoires. Er gehört zu den wichtigsten Interpreten des deutschen romantischen Liedes. Sein Projekt *Song of America* in Zusammenarbeit mit der Library of Congress fördert die Verbreitung und Erforschung des amerikanischen Liedgutes. Mit der 2003 gegründeten Hampsong Foundation unterstützt er interkulturellen Dialog und Verständigung mit dem Mittel des Kunstliedes.

Als leidenschaftlicher Lehrer wurde er kürzlich in die Amerikanische Akademie der Künste und Wissenschaften aufgenommen.

Louise Kerz Hirschfeld

Honorary Piscator Award, American Theater Historian and Curator
Piscator Ehrenpreis, Amerikanische Theaterhistorikerin und Kuratorin

Louise Kerz Hirschfeld is President of the Al Hirschfeld Foundation, honoring her late husband, the longtime theater illustrator and caricaturist of the New York Times. She has curated various exhibitions, such as *Hirschfeld on Shaw*, and *Hirschfeld on Tennessee Williams*, and is collaborating with the New York City Board of Education to produce *The Al Hirschfeld Project*, a curriculum for teaching the arts in New York public schools. In 2010, she married Lewis B. Cullman.

Louise Kerz Hirschfeld ist Präsidentin der Al Hirschfeld Stiftung, die das Erbe ihres verstorbenen Mannes, des Theaterzeichners und Karikaturisten der New York Times, pflegt. Sie hat diverse Ausstellungen kuratiert, etwa *Hirschfeld über Shaw* und *Hirschfeld über Tennessee Williams* und erarbeitet mit dem Schulamt der Stadt New York das *Al Hirschfeld Projekt*, einen Studienplan für den Unterricht der Künste an den öffentlichen Schulen New Yorks. 2010 heiratete sie Lewis B. Cullman.

Lewis B. Cullman

Honorary Piscator Award, American Entrepreneur and Philanthropist
Piscator Ehrenpreis, Amerikanischer Unternehmer und Mäzen

Lewis B. Cullman, the engineer of the first leveraged buyout, is "one of the nation's major and most generous philanthropists" (Walter Cronkite). He and his late wife Dorothy have given away over $ 223 million to charity. He serves on many boards and is Chairman emeritus of *Chess in the Schools*, which has taught chess to close to 500.000 economically disadvantaged inner-city children, helping them to develop decision-making and social skills.

Lewis B. Cullman, Pionier des Leveraged Buy-Out, ist „einer der bedeutendsten und großzügigsten Mäzene der Nation" (Walter Cronkite). Er und seine verstorbene Frau Dorothy spendeten bislang mehr als $ 223 Millionen. Er war jahrelang Vorsitzender von *Schach in den Schulen*, einer Organisation die bisher 500.000 Schülern aus wirtschaftlich schwachen Familien das Schachspiel lehrte und so ihre soziale Kompetenz stärkte.

1 Lewis B. Cullman (center), with the Academy Award-winning set and costume designer Tony Walton (right) and his wife Gen

2 Gallery owners Achim Moeller (left), and Erik Thomsen (center), with Heather Randall

3 Gregorij von Leïtis (left) welcomes the Lithuanian Consul General Valdemaras Sarapinas (center) and his Czech colleague Eliska Zigova

4 The Consul General of Austria in New York, Dr. Ernst-Peter Brezovszky, talks with baritone Thomas Hampson, and the composer and long-time President of the Manhattan School of Music Robert Sirota (from left)

5 Adele Chatfield-Taylor, President of the American Academy in Rome, with Lewis B. Cullman and his grand-daughter Mia Cullman (from left)

6 Lya Friedrich Pfeifer (left), and New York Times Reporter Enid Nemy

1 Lewis B. Cullman (Mitte), mit dem Oskar-Preisgekrönten Bühnen- und Kostumbildner Tony Walton (rechts) und dessen Frau Gen

2 Die Galeristen Achim Moeller (links) und Erik Thomsen (Mitte) mit Heather Randall

3 Gregorij von Leïtis (links) begrüßt den litauischen Generalkonsul Valdemaras Sarapinas (Mitte) und dessen tschechische Kollegin Eliska Zigova

4 Österreichs Generalkonsul in New York Dr. Ernst-Peter Brezovszky unterhält sich vor der Preisverleihung am 14. März 2012 mit dem Bariton Thomas Hampson und dem Komponisten und langjährigen Präsidenten der Manhattan School of Music Robert Sirota (v.l.n.r.)

5 Adele Chatfield-Taylor, Präsidentin der American Academy in Rom, mit Lewis B. Cullman und dessen Enkelin Mia Cullman (v.l.n.r.)

6 Lya Friedrich Pfeifer (links) und New York Times Reporterin Enid Nemy

7 Dr. Antje-Katrin Kühnemann (right), physician, TV moderator and advisor to The Lahr von Leïtis Academy & Archive, who came specifically from Germany to the 25th Piscator Award Luncheon, talks with Henry H. Arnhold

8 The Dance Critic Jennifer Homans, author of the bestseller *Apollo's Angels: A History of Ballet*, Frank Hentschker, Director of the Martin E. Segal Theater Center at City University New York, Dr. Monika Kalista, and Christopher Dingstad (from right)

9 Meera T. Gandhi (center), with Patty Raynes Davis (left), and Richard Turley

10 Thomas Hampson (center) showing the audience the Award Certificate, which he has just received from the hands of Gregorij von Leïtis (left), after Robert Sirota had introduced him

11 The Honorary Piscator Award Recipients of 2012, the couple Louise Kerz Hirschfeld (center) and Lewis B. Cullman (2nd from right) sourrounded by their speakers Adele Chatfield-Taylor (left) and Tony Walton (right), as well as Gregorij von Leïtis

12 Louise Kerz Hirschfeld (left) with photographer Carin Drechsler-Marx

7 Dr. Antje-Katrin Kühnemann (rechts), Ärztin, Fernsehmoderatorin und Mitglied des Beirats von The Lahr von Leïtis Academy & Archive, die eigens aus Deutschland zur 25. Preisverleihung angereist war, unterhält sich angeregt mit Henry H. Arnhold

8 Die Tanz-Kritikerin Jennifer Homans, Autorin des Bestsellers *Apollo's Angels: A History of Ballet*, Frank Hentschker, Direktor des Martin E. Segal Theater Center der City University New York, Hofrätin Dr. Monika Kalista und Christopher Dingstad (v.r.n.l.)

9 Meera T. Gandhi (Mitte), mit Patty Raynes Davis (links) und Richard Turley

10 Thomas Hampson (Mitte) präsentiert dem Publikum die Preisurkunde, die er aus den Händen von Gregorij von Leïtis (links) erhalten hat, nachdem Robert Sirota die Laudatio gehalten hatte

11 Die Ehrenpreisträger 2012, das Ehepaar Louise Kerz Hirschfeld (Mitte) und Lewis B. Cullman (2.v.r.) im Kreis ihrer Laudatoren Adele Chatfield-Taylor (links) und Tony Walton (rechts), sowie Gregorij von Leïtis

12 Louise Kerz Hirschfeld (links) mit der Photographin Carin Drechsler-Marx

» I am a passionate Germanophile, and I found a great deal of my understanding of life in general and the humanities specifically, through the literature of Germany. There is a word in German that is not translatable, and yet may be the lifeline that we all believe in in this room. And that word is *Bildung*. […] Bildung for me means that you cherish the idea that tomorrow you will know more about why you are alive than you know today. And that is a very special thing. There is a story about little Jonny in the classroom having a nap in one of his classes in the back. The teacher is trying to raise children's, students' ideas of civics, civil responsibility, democracy … all those things. And Jonny is really not all there. And she goes and knocks: "Jonny, Jonny, wake up! And Jonny says: "What?" And the teacher says: "Jonny I want you to explain to me one time. Just give me the definition: What is the difference between ignorance and apathy?" And Jonny yawns and says: "I don't know! And I really don't care!" […]

I think the problem of this little joke has gone way too far in our mutual cultures […] It's not just: I don't know and I don't care! It's now become: I don't care if I don't know. And we are in terrible times, as far as I am concerned. And I don't mean to ruin this lunch by any means. I want to galvanize our collective spirits today! But never should we possibly assume that this will take care of itself. The evidence of our political dialogue today is horrifying, as we must all agree it is. And I'm not talking about Republicans and Democrats. I am talking about political, the real political dialogue in this country. It's based on emotions and ignorance. It revels about what is not known and cherishes what shouldn't be talked.

This is no path for this country. This is no path out of this malaise of fear and misunderstanding of most cultures, but first and foremost our own. If we do not embrace the heart of liberal arts education, the humanities and letters, the path and belief in the ideals that gave us this wonderful country, that allows us to agree and disagree …. I have been so proud for so many years of explaining the essential phenomenon of American culture: You can vehemently disagree with one another at a table, and you invite that person for coffee afterwards. We are starting to lose that, because we start to lose our connection to the arts and humanities. […]

It is exactly clubs like this, people like us who are devoted in their walks of life that know: there is a deeper blueprint of who we are as human beings in the prism of our cultures in which we communicate to one another. And most of this communication is found in the language of poetry and the language of music. And this communication we should cherish. […] We have unravelled the liberal arts' embracing of that difference. I think that our great motto "In pluribus unum" is about pluribus not homogenization. Unum does not mean to become of the same mind. It means to embrace the diversity of our individualism and go without fear where we know we must go … together. That's the future. – Thank you! «

Thomas Hampson
Excerpts from his extemporaneous speech in
acceptance of the award

» Ich bin ein leidenschaftlicher Freund des Deutschen und verdanke einen Großteil meiner Einsicht ins Leben im Allgemeinen und in die Geisteswissenschaften im Besonderen der deutschen Literatur.

Es gibt ein deutsches Wort, das nicht übersetzt werden kann, das aber die Lebensader dessen bezeichnet, woran wir alle in diesem Raum glauben. Dieses Wort ist *Bildung*. [...] Für mich bedeutet Bildung, dass wir die Idee wertschätzen, morgen mehr darüber zu wissen, warum wir leben, als heute. Und das ist eine ganz besondere Angelegenheit. Es gibt eine Geschichte vom kleinen Jonny, der hinten im Klassenraum während des Unterrichts ein Nickerchen hält. Die Lehrerin bemüht sich gerade, in Sozialkunde das Bewusstsein der Schüler für bürgerschaftliches Engagement, Demokratie und so weiter zu stärken. Aber Jonny ist überhaupt nicht bei der Sache. Die Lehrerin geht zu ihm hin und rüttelt ihn: „Jonny, wach auf!" „Was ist denn?" fragt Jonny. Die Lehrerin sagt: „Jonny, ich möchte, dass Du mir erklärst, was der Unterschied zwischen Unkenntnis und Teilnahmslosigkeit ist." Jonny gähnt und antwortet: „Ich weiß es nicht! Und es interessiert mich auch nicht!" [...]

Ich denke, das Problem, das dieser kleine Witz benennt, hat sich in unserer gemeinsamen Kultur viel zu sehr breit gemacht. [...] Es ist nicht mehr nur die Haltung: Ich weiß es nicht, und es interessiert mich nicht! Es ist die Einstellung: Mir ist egal, wenn ich es nicht weiß.

Wir leben in schrecklichen Zeiten – so empfinde ich es. Und ich möchte Ihnen dieses Festmahl nicht verderben. Ich möchte unseren Gemeinschaftssinn wachrütteln! Wir sollten nicht annehmen, dass das Problem sich von selbst erledigen wird. Der Zustand unseres politischen Dialogs heute ist grauenerregend, wie wir alle zugeben müssen. Und ich spreche nicht über Republikaner und Demokraten. Ich meine die politische Debatte in diesem Land. Sie ist geleitet von Gefühl und Ignoranz. Sie verstrickt sich in das, was unbekannt ist, und hält sich mit Dingen auf, über die man nicht sprechen sollte.

Dies ist nicht der Weg für dieses Land. Dieser Weg führt nicht heraus aus der Maläse von Furcht und Missverständnis, die in den meisten Kulturen grassiert, aber vor allem in unserer eigenen. Wir müssen uns kümmern um die freien Künste, die Geisteswissenschaften, wir müssen uns den Weg und den Glauben an die Ideale zu eigen machen, aus denen dieses wundervolle Land hervorgegangen ist; Ideale, die uns erlauben, verschiedener Meinung zu sein… Viele Jahre lang habe ich voller Stolz das Kernphänomen amerikanischer Kultur erläutert: Wir können heftige Meinungsverschiedenheiten haben um den Tisch und später die andere Person zum Kaffee einladen. Wir fangen an, genau dies zu verlieren, weil wir dabei sind, unsere Verbindung mit den Künsten und Humanwissenschaften zu verlieren [...]

Clubs wie dieser und Menschen wie Sie, die im Leben engagiert sind, wissen: In der Vielfalt der Kulturen, in der wir miteinander kommunizieren, liegt unserem Menschsein ein tieferer Entwurf zugrunde. Ein Großteil dieser interkulturellen Kommunikation findet sich in der Sprache der Dichtung und der Musik. Und dieses Zwiegespräch sollten wir in Ehren halten. [...] Wir haben das von den freien Künsten gelehrte Wertschätzen dieser Vielfalt zerstört. Unser großer Leitspruch „In pluribus unum" betont die Vielfalt nicht die Gleichmacherei. Unum heißt nicht, dass wir alle der gleichen Meinung sind. Es bedeutet, dass wir die Vielfalt unseres Individualismus akzeptieren und furchtlos dorthin gehen, wo wir hingehen müssen … gemeinsam. Das ist die Zukunft. – Vielen Dank! «

Thomas Hampson
Auszug aus seiner improvisierten Dankesrede

» It was 1961 … Maria Piscator descended the grand Staircase at the Frankfurter Hof Hotel. She was a vision of elegance in a beige flowing dress, and practically danced down the steps… one beautiful arched foot after another.

There was a festive luncheon, as my first husband Leo Kerz shared theatrical news from Broadway with his old teacher and mentor, the director Erwin Piscator. Leo Kerz produced and designed Ionesco's absurdist play *Rhinoceros* and the New York production was a great hit. I listened attentively as they also gossiped about the Dramatic Workshop at the New School in the early 1940s.

In Berlin several years later, Piscator stepped out of virtual retirement and directed *The Deputy*, the play about Pope Pius' silence during World War II.

Leo Kerz designed the sets and costumes. We attended a meeting at the director's stylish apartment off the Kurfürstendamm; he proudly showed us the décor which Maria had selected for his home. There were photo murals of his great productions, *The Good Soldier Schwejk* and the lovely actress Dolly Haas in *The Chalk Circle.*

The Deputy became an international success, although the young author Rolf Hochhuth was angered when his play was cut from eight to three hours.
The Berlin mayor, Willy Brandt, assured Piscator the play would open in spite of protests from the Vatican, and the Krupp organization. Police guarded the theater on opening night, and the German audiences wept throughout the play. At the end there was silence… and then an eruption of applause as the creative team appeared on stage.
So in 1963, Erwin Piscator reappeared in Berlin as the leader of the political and documentary theater. But he and his work was never far from the trenches of World War I where he became a pacifist.

We mourned with Maria when Piscator died… Eventually she continued to run her salon for European émigrés and friends. There were fascinating evenings; German, French and Russian accents permeated the 19th century décor. Champagne and delicate "Vorspeisen" were served. But the main topics of conversation were around old memories, days long gone by, interrupted by the worst possible human tragedy – ignited by World War II. Prince Romanov recounted his days in Paris after the Russian Revolution, Leo Kerz, as a student in Berlin sanctified Piscator's great productions of the 1920s. Writer Hans Sahl translated Arthur Miller's plays for German audiences in the 1950s and Judith Malina reviewed her time at the Dramatic Workshop with Julian Beck. A young director, Gregorij von Leïtis, was also there. At the center of everything – the elegant Maria Piscator, Reinhardt ballerina and graduate of the Sorbonne, toast of Vienna and Paris, exemplified European sophistication for all of us. Thank you for this award. «

Louise Kerz Hirschfeld
Excerpts from her acceptance speech

» Es was 1961 … Maria Piscator schritt die große Treppe im Hotel Frankfurter Hof hinab. Sie war eine Erscheinung der Eleganz in ihrem beigen fließenden Kleid, und tanzte gewissermaßen die Stufen herab… einen schönen gewölbten Fuß nach dem anderen.

Wir hatten ein geselliges Mittagessen, bei dem mein erster Mann Leo Kerz Neuigkeiten vom Broadway mit seinem alten Lehrer und Mentor, dem Regisseur Erwin Piscator austauschte. Leo Kerz führte Regie und besorgte die Ausstattung von Ionescos absurdem Stück *Die Nashörner* und die New Yorker Produktion war ein großer Erfolg. Ich hörte aufmerksam zu, wie sie plauderten über den Dramatic Workshop an der New School in den frühen 1940er Jahren.

Einige Jahre später in Berlin folgte Piscator dem Ruf gleichsam aus dem Ruhestand heraus und inszenierte *Der Stellvertreter,* jenes Stück über das Schweigen von Papst Pius XII. während des 2. Weltkrieges.

Leo Kerz gestaltete das Bühnenbild und die Kostüme. Wir hatten eine Besprechung in Piscators stilvoller Wohnung unweit vom Kurfürstendamm; voller Stolz zeigte er uns die Inneneinrichtung, die Maria für sein Zuhause ausgesucht hatte. Die Wände waren voller Photos von seinen großen Produktionen, *Der brave Soldat Schwejk* und die reizende Schauspielerin Dolly Haas im *Kreidekreis.*

Der Stellvertreter wurde international ein Erfolg, obwohl der junge Schriftsteller Rolf Hochhuth wütend war, als sein Stück von acht auf drei Stunden gekürzt wurde.
Berlins Bürgermeister Willy Brandt versicherte Piscator, dass das Stück herauskommen würde trotz der Proteste des Vatikans und der Firma Krupp. Die Polizei bewachte das Theater während der Premiere, und das deutsche Publikum weinte während des ganzen Stückes. Am Ende war es ganz still… und dann Begeisterungsstürme, als das künstlerische Team auf der Bühne erschien.

So trat Piscator 1963 in Berlin erneut als der Vertreter des politischen Dokumentartheaters in Erscheinung. Aber er und sein Werk waren niemals weit entfernt von den Schützengräben des 1. Weltkrieges, in denen er zum Pazifisten geworden war.

Wir trauerten mit Maria, als Piscator starb… Schließlich führte Maria ihren Salon für die europäischen Emigranten und Freunde fort. Es waren faszinierende Abende: Deutsche, französische und russische Akzente durchzogen das im Stil des 19. Jahrhunderts dekorierte Apartment. Champagner und köstliche Vorspeisen wurden serviert. Doch das Gespräch kreiste immer wieder um alte Erinnerungen, längst vergangene Tage, die durch die schlimmste Tragödie der Menschheit jäh unterbrochen wurden – ausgelöst durch den 2. Weltkrieg. Prinz Romanow erzählte von seinen Tagen in Paris nach der russischen Revolution, Leo Kerz, damals Student in Paris, glorifizierte Piscators große Inszenierungen aus den 1920er Jahren. Schriftsteller Hans Sahl übersetzte Arthur Millers Stücke in den 1950er Jahren fürs deutsche Publikum, und Judith Malina ließ ihre Zeit im Dramatic Workshop mit Julian Beck Revue passieren. Da war auch ein junger Regisseur, Gregorij von Leïtis. Im Mittelpunkt stand die elegante Maria Piscator, Ballerina bei Max Reinhardt, Absolventin der Sorbonne, in Wien und Paris gefeiert. Sie verkörperte für uns alle europäische Raffinesse. Vielen Dank für diesen Preis. «

Louise Kerz Hirschfeld
Auszug aus ihrer Dankesrede

2013

André Bishop

Piscator Award, American Theater Impresario
Piscator Preis, Amerikanischer Theaterimpresario

André Bishop, Artistic Director of Lincoln Center Theater since January 1992, and Producing Artistic Director since July 2013, has developed and produced new plays and musicals by many of America's leading playwrights, composers and lyricists. Prior to his arrival at Lincoln Center, Bishop served as Playwrights Horizon's Artistic Director for ten years and as its Literary Manager for six.

His many successful productions at that theater included three Pulitzer Prize winners: *The Heidi Chronicles, Driving Miss Daisy*, and *Sunday in the Park with George.*

As Lincoln Center Theater's Producing Artistic Director, Bishop is responsible for the continuing Playwrights Program, a series of readings and workshops devised to develop new work and foster new artists. With Bernard Gersten and Dramaturg Anne Cattaneo, he started Lincoln Center Theater's Directors Lab, which supports and nurtures the work of approximately one hundred young directors each year in a laboratory setting. He was recently inducted into the Theater Hall of Fame.

André Bishop, seit 1992 Intendant des Lincoln Center Theater und seit Juli 2013 Producing Artistic Director, hat geholfen, viele neue Stücke und Musicals von Amerikas führenden Dramatikern, Komponisten und Textern zu entwickeln und aufzuführen. Zuvor war Bishop zehn Jahre Intendant und sechs Jahre Literaturmanger von Playwrights Horizons, einer Non-Profit-Organisation, die zum New Yorker Off-Broadway gehört.

Zu seinen vielen erfolgreichen Produktionen dort gehören drei mit dem Pulitzer Preis ausgezeichnete Stücke: *The Heidi Chronicles, Miss Daisy und ihr Chauffeur*, und *Sunday in the Park with George.*

Als Producing Artistic Director des Lincoln Center Theater ist Bishop verantwortlich für das Dramatiker-Programm, eine Serie von Lesungen und Workshops zur Förderung junger Künstler. Mit Bernard Gersten und Dramaturgin Anne Cattaneo startete er das Lincoln Center Theater's Directors Lab, das jährlich in einem experimentellen Rahmen die Arbeit von etwa 100 angehenden Regisseuren unterstützt. André Bishop wurde kürzlich in die Theater Hall of Fame aufgenommen.

Barbara Goldsmith

Honorary Piscator Award, American Writer, Historian, and Philanthropist
Piscator Ehrenpreis, Amerikanische Schriftstellerin, Historikerin und Mäzenin

Barbara Goldsmith – whose books have been praised as "thoroughly researched and beautifully written … a brilliant synthesis and masterful biographical writing" (Joan Hendrick) – was born in New York City.

Her latest book *Obsessive Genius: The Inner World of Marie Curie* has been translated into twenty-one languages. It is based on the workbooks, letters and diaries of Polish physicist and chemist Marie Curie.

Barbara Goldsmith spearheaded a campaign to preserve our written heritage by convincing US publishers to use only permanent paper that lasts 300 years instead of disintegrating in 30.

She founded and funds the *Barbara Goldsmith / PEN Freedom to Write Awards* that consistently turn the media spotlight on writers imprisoned for expressing their views and has invariably seen them released. Of the 37 writers imprisoned, missing or tortured at the time of her award, 34 were set free.

The *Barbara Goldsmith / PEN Freedom to Write Award* was instrumental in starting the campaign that led to the Chinese writer Liu Xiaobo winning the 2010 Nobel Peace Prize.

Barbara Goldsmith, deren Bücher gepriesen werden als "gründlich recherchiert und wunderbar geschrieben… eine brillante Synthese und meisterhafte biographische Schreibkunst" (Joan Hendrick), ist gebürtige New Yorkerin.

Ihr jüngstes Buch *Marie Curie: Die erste Frau der Wissenschaft* wurde in 21 Sprachen übersetzt. Es basiert auf den Notizen, Briefen und Tagebüchern der polnischen Physikerin und Chemikerin Marie Curie.

Barbara Goldsmith führte eine Kampagne an zur Erhaltung unseres schriftlichen Erbes: Sie überzeugte US-Verleger, nur dauerhaftes Papier zu benutzen, das 300 Jahre hält, statt nach 30 Jahren zu zerfallen.

Sie gründete und finanziert den *Barbara Goldsmith / PEN Freedom To Write Preis.* Durch ihn wird regelmäßig die Aufmerksamkeit der Medien auf Schriftsteller gelenkt, die eingesperrt wurden, weil sie ihre Sicht der Dinge äußerten. Von den 37 Schriftstellern, die den Preis erhielten, während sie im Gefängnis saßen, als vermisst galten, oder gefoltert wurden, wurden 34 freigelassen.

Der *Barbara Goldsmith / PEN Freedom to Write Award* trug maßgeblich dazu bei, dass der chinesische Schriftsteller Liu Xiaobo 2010 den Friedensnobelpreis gewann.

1 Elysium's board member Jolana Blau (left); John Morning, member of the New York State Council on the Arts (center) who brought with him a message from Governor Andrew M. Cuomo, and Gregorij von Leïtis

2 Chev. Cesare L. Santeramo, Marcelo Dos Santos, Dr. Robert J. Campbell, and Anne Benôit (from left)

3 Eve Queler (left), Founder and Artistic Director Emeritus of the Opera Orchestra of New York, with Luna Kaufman

4 Alexandra Kauka (2nd from right), Advisor to Elysium and The Lahr von Leïtis Academy & Archive, with her guests Uta von Dalwigk-Machatius (left), Nikolaus von Dalwigk (2nd from left), and Barbara Countess von Wolff-Metternich

5 Kathleen A. Moskal McCord, the Czech Consul General in New York Martin Dvořák; Ladislav Steinhübel, First Secretary at the Czech Permanent Mission to the UN, and Mercedes Mestre (from left)

6 Dr. Vartan Gregorian (left), President of the Carnegie Corporation in New York, one of America's biggest and most influential foundations, in conversation with Gregorij von Leïtis

1 Elysiums Vorstandsmitglied Jolana Blau (links), John Morning, Direktoriumsmitglied des New York State Council on the Arts (Mitte), der eine Botschaft vom Gouverneur des Staates New York Andrew M. Cuomo überbrachte, und Gregorij von Leïtis

2 Chev. Cesare L. Santeramo, Marcelo Dos Santos, Dr. Robert J. Campbell und Anne Benôit (v.l.n.r.)

3 Eve Queler (links), Gründerin und emeritierte Intendantin des Opera Orchestra of New York, mit Luna Kaufman

4 Alexandra Kauka (2.v.r.), Beiratsmitglied von Elysium und The Lahr von Leïtis Academy & Archive, mit ihren Gästen Uta von Dalwigk-Machatius (links), Nikolaus von Dalwigk (2.v.l.) und Barbara Gräfin von Wolff-Metternich

5 Kathleen A. Moskal McCord, der tschechische Generalkonsul Martin Dvořák, erster Sekretär der Tschechischen Ständigen Vertretung bei den Vereinten Nationen, und Mercedes Mestre (v.l.n.r.)

6 Dr. Vartan Gregorian (links), Präsident der Carnegie Corporation in New York, einer der größten und einflußreichsten amerikanischen Stiftungen, im Gespräch mit Gregorij von Leïtis

7 Katrin Kalden (right), and Rolf H. Heitmeyer

8 Dagmar Trippen, the Deputy Consul General of Germany Dr. Oliver Schnakenberg, and Cornelia Thomsen (from left)

9 Two of Barbara Goldsmith' close friends, philanthropist Mica Ertegün (left), and literary agent Lynn Nesbit (right), in conversation with Olaf Unsoeld

10 Author and biographer Patricia Bosworth, Elysium's board member Oliver Ott Trumbo II, and Barbara Goldsmith's daughter Alice Elgart (from left)

11 Barbara Goldsmith (center) gave a spontaneous acceptance speech, after having received the Honorary Piscator Award from Gregorij von Leitis (left). In his remarks Dr. Vartan Gregorian praised the extraordinary achievements of Barbara Goldsmith and called her "a cultural icon in New York"

12 André Bishop (left) holding the Erwin Piscator Award 2013, which he has just received from Gregorij H. von Leitis (center). Theater and opera director Bartlett Sher introduced André Bishop

7 Katrin Kalden (rechts) und Rolf H. Heitmeyer

8 Dagmar Trippen, der stellvertretende deutsche Generalkonsul Dr. Oliver Schnakenberg und Cornelia Thomsen (v.l.n.r.)

9 Zwei von Barbara Goldsmith' engen Freundinnen, die Mäzenin Mica Ertegün (links) und die Literaturagentin Lynn Nesbit (rechts) im Gespräch mit Olaf Unsoeld

10 Die Autorin Patricia Bosworth, Elysiums US-Vorstandsmitglied Oliver Ott Trumbo II und Barbara Goldsmith' Tochter Alice Elgart (v.l.n.r.)

11 Barbara Goldsmith (Mitte) hält eine spontane Dankesrede, nachdem sie aus den Händen von Gregorij H. von Leitis (links) den Ehrenpreis erhalten hat. In seiner Laudatio preist Dr. Vartan Gregorian die außergewöhnlichen Verdienste von Barbara Goldsmith und nennt sie "eine kulturelle Ikone in New York"

12 André Bishop (links) hält die Urkunde des Erwin Piscator Preises 2013 in Händen, die er gerade von Gregorij von Leitis (Mitte) überreicht bekommen hat. Der Theater- und Opernregisseur Bartlett Sher hielt die Laudatio auf André Bishop

STATE OF NEW YORK

EXECUTIVE CHAMBER

ALBANY 12224

ANDREW M. CUOMO
GOVERNOR

March 12, 2013

Dear Friends:

It is a pleasure to send greetings to everyone gathered for the 26th Annual Erwin Piscator Award Ceremony hosted by Elysium - Between Two Continents.

The Empire State is fortunate to be home to organizations that build bridges of international friendship through the shared exchange of art, culture and academia. Since 1983, Elysium has been committed to preserving the music, drama, and literature produced by European artists, including many who suffered during World War II. This rare art reflects the unique perspective of those who lived through a difficult era and, today, is treasured by all the world for its profound historical and social significance.

Tonight, you celebrate the creative spirit of noted theatrical pioneer Erwin Piscator, and honor two individuals who reflect his passion for all forms of artistic expression. I join in congratulating André Bishop and Barbara Goldsmith for their significant contributions to the world of music and literature.

Best wishes for an enjoyable and memorable occasion.

Sincerely,

ANDREW M. CUOMO

Grußwort des Gouverneurs des Staates New York
Andrew M. Cuomo, New York, 12. März 2013

Liebe Freunde,

es ist mir eine Freude, Grüße zu übermitteln an alle, die zur 26. Jährlichen Erwin Piscator Preisverleihung durch Elysium – Between Two Continents versammelt sind.

Der Empire State hat das Glück, Heimat zu sein für Organisationen, die durch den gelebten Austausch von Kunst, Kultur und Bildung Brücken internationaler Freundschaft bauen. Seit 1983 hat sich Elysium der Aufgabe verschrieben, Musik, Theater und Literatur zu bewahren, die von europäischen Künstlern geschaffen wurde. Dazu gehören die vielen Künstler, die während des 2. Weltkrieges gelitten haben. Diese seltene Kunst reflektiert die einzigartige Sichtweise derer, die eine schwierige Geschichtsepoche durchlebt haben. Heute werden diese Kunstwerke wegen ihrer tiefen historischen und sozialen Aussagekraft rund um die Welt hoch geschätzt.

Heute feiern Sie den kreativen Geist des renommierten Theaterpioniers Erwin Pisccator und ehren zwei Persönlichkeiten, die seine Leidenschaft für jedwede Form künstlerischen Ausdrucks teilen. Mit Ihnen beglückwünsche ich André Bishop und Barbara Goldsmith für ihre bedeutenden Beiträge im Bereich Musik und Literatur.

Beste Wünsche für einen angenehmen und denkwürdigen Festakt.

Mit freundlichen Grüßen,

Andrew M. Cuomo

Übersetzung: Michael Lahr

» The most important thing about André [...] is his radical accomplishment of his devotion to new writers, new and young writers. Tirelessly he supported their cause to the point that when he came to take his job at Lincoln Center Theater he had written in his contract, that they must build a new theater exclusively devoted to young writers. You might say that this is prodigal, but he had it that this work would be available to everybody at a very very cheap ticket price. [...] When I try to think of the radical gesture of that: Here the most powerful theater in America, led with enormous love and dignity, to make works of importance at the grandest cultural scale of Lincoln Center at the cheapest possible price, I think that this kind of subversiveness is absolutely the child of Erwin Piscator. «

Bartlett Sher
Excerpts from his remarks on André Bishop

» I am convinced that we are living in a golden age of the American theater, mostly because of our playwrights. [...]
I have and I've always had two wishes for the health of the theater and its writers in this still new century:
One is that audiences come to new work with open hearts and minds, not to form an opinion or to make a judgement, but to have an experience.
And secondly and probably even most important: Let us not take our artists, any of our artists, even our producers, for granted. Because we have such a rich display of talent in this country we tend to believe that talent will go on flourishing forever. It won't, unless those among us, who love the theater, indeed who love all the arts, see ourselves as devoted caretakers. «

André Bishop
Excerpts from his acceptance speech

» Barbara is a cultural icon in New York. Even though few of us were given the status of "living landmark", in her case I prefer the selection of an icon. Because landmarks often are neglected, they are subject to depletion, they are forgotten, but icons always have to be revisited. [...] Barbara has moral and intellectual integrity and honesty. She is one of the most decent human beings, I have known. Barbara is dedicated to her family, her friends and her causes. Causes include ... freedom, intellectual integrity, knowledge but most importantly social justice and to do the right thing. Throughout her life she has done the right thing. That's why she is an icon for me and for many others. «

Dr. Vartan Gregorian
Excerpts from his remarks on Barbara Goldsmith

» I'd like to say a little bit about why human rights and PEN / Barbara Goldsmith Awards tie in with the theater and with everything. It's because of word of mouth, it's because theatrical people the world over are the first to be persecuted when terrible regimes come to power. They don't want ideas, they want someone who will quietly follow. [...] Freedom to write is about helping these people get out of jail, to not be tortured, not disappear. [...] You have to have the willingness to wake up at two in the morning when someone calls with an emergency and says "You know who. Get on your computer and write him a letter." There are so many things you have to do to be a real part of PEN. «

Barbara Goldsmith
Excerpts from her acceptance speech

» Das Wichtigste an André ist seine fundamentale Leistung in seiner Hinwendung zu neuen Schriftstellern, neuen und jungen Dramatikern. Unermüdlich hat er ihre Sache unterstützt, bis zu dem Punkt, dass er sich vertraglich zusichern ließ, bevor er die Leitung des Lincoln Center Theater übernahm, dass man ein neues Theater bauen werde, welches ausschließlich jungen Stückeschreibern gewidmet ist. Sie mögen es für verschwenderisch halten, doch er bestand darauf, dass diese Aufführungen für jeden zugänglich seien zu einem sehr günstigen Eintrittspreis. [...] Wenn ich mir die Radikalität dieser Geste vor Augen führe: Hier haben Sie das einflußreichste amerikanische Theater, das mit großer Hingabe und Wertschätzung wichtige Produktionen im Rampenlicht des Lincoln Center zum billigstmöglichen Preis auf die Bühne bringt ... ich bin davon überzeugt, daß diese Art von Subversion ganz das geistige Kind eines Erwin Piscator ist. «

Bartlett Sher
Auszug aus seiner Laudatio auf André Bishop

» Ich bin davon überzeugt, daß wir in einem goldenen Zeitalter des amerikanischen Theaters leben, besonders wegen unserer Dramatiker. Ich hatte und habe zwei Wünsche für das Wohl des Theaters und seiner Schriftsteller in diesem noch jungen Jahrhundert: Erstens, daß das Publikum sich neue Stücke mit offenen Herzen und unvoreingenommenem Geist anschaut, nicht um sich eine Meinung zu bilden oder ein Urteil, sondern um eine Erfahrung zu machen. Und zweitens - und dies ist vielleicht noch wichtiger: Betrachten wir unsere Künstler, alle Künstler, auch unsere Regisseure, nicht als eine Selbstverständlichkeit. Weil wir so einen reichen Fundus an Talent hier haben, neigen wir dazu zu glauben, daß dieses Talent immer weiter blühen wird. Dem ist nicht so! Es sei denn, daß diejenigen unter uns, die das Theater lieben, ja die die Künste überhaupt lieben, sich als hingebungsvolle Hüter erweisen. «

André Bishop
Auszug aus seiner Dankesrede

» Barbara ist eine kulturelle Ikone in New York. Obwohl ihr von der Denkmalschutzbehörde der Titel einer "lebenden Sehenswürdigkeit" verliehen wurde, bevorzuge ich den Begriff einer Ikone. Sehenswürdigkeiten werden oft vernachlässigt, sie sind dem Verfall heimgegeben, sie werden vergessen, aber Ikonen werden stets von Neuem aufgesucht. [...] Barbara besitzt moralische und intellektuelle Integrität und Aufrichtigkeit. Sie ist eine der anständigsten Menschen, die ich kenne. Barbara widmet sich ganz ihrer Familie, ihren Freunden und ihren Anliegen. Intellektuelle Freiheit und Integrität, Wissensvermittlung liegen ihr am Herzen, aber besonders wichtig ist ihr soziale Gerechtigkeit und das Richtige zu tun. Während ihres ganzen Lebens hat sie immer das Richtige getan. Darum ist sie für mich und für viele andere eine Ikone. «

Dr. Vartan Gregorian
Auszug aus seiner Laudatio auf Barbara Goldsmith

» Ich möchte ein wenig erklären, warum die Menschenrechte und der PEN / Barbara Goldsmith Preis mit dem Theater zusammenhängen: Weil Theaterleute auf der ganzen Welt zu den Ersten gehören, die verfolgt werden, wenn fürchterliche Regime an die Macht kommen. Solche Regime wollen keine Ideen, sie wollen Menschen, die stillschweigend gehorchen. Freedom to write will eben diesen Menschen helfen, aus dem Gefängnis frei zu kommen, nicht gefoltert zu werden, nicht verschleppt zu werden. [...] Man muß bereit sein, um zwei Uhr morgens aufzustehen, wenn jemand in einer Notlage anruft und sagt: „Du kennst doch den und den. Setz Dich an den Computer und schreib ihm einen Brief." Es gibt viel zu tun, wenn man wirklich ein Teil von PEN sein will. «

Barbara Goldsmith
Auszug aus ihrer Dankesrede

Elysium – between two continents
Fostering artistic and creative dialogue and mutual friendship between the United States of America and Europe.
Künstlerischer Dialog, schöpferischer Austausch und Freundschaft zwischen Europa und den USA.

www.elysiumbtc.org

The Lahr von Leïtis Academy & Archive
Art and Education without borders. Education and knowledge as efficient tools to fight against ignorance, discrimination, and hatred.
Kunst und Bildung ohne Grenzen. Wissensvermittlung und Weiterbildung als effektive Werkzeuge im Kampf gegen Ignoranz, Diskriminierung und Haß.

www.lahrvonleitisacademy.eu

Gregorij von Leïtis
Founder and Artistic Director of Elysium and President of The Lahr von Leïtis Academy & Archive, has been working in the theater for over 40 years. In 2003 he was awarded the Knight's Cross of Merit of the Federal Republic of Germany for his achievements in promoting understanding between peoples by way of art. In 1985 he received, as the first non-American, the New York Theatre Club Prize. In 1983 he founded the Elysium Theater Company in New York, which in 1993 was rededicated as Elysium – between two continents. He is Chairman of the Erwin Piscator Award, which he founded in 1985.

Gründer und Intendant von Elysium und Präsident von The Lahr von Leïtis Academy & Archive, ist seit über 40 Jahren im Theater tätig. Für seine Verdienste um die Förderung der Völkerverständigung mit den Mitteln der Kunst wurde ihm 2003 das Bundesverdienstkreuz verliehen. 1985 erhielt er als erster Nicht-Amerikaner den New York Theatre Club Prize. 1983 gründete er in New York die Elysium Theater Company, aus der 1993 Elysium – between two continents hervorging. 1985 rief er den Erwin Piscator Preis ins Leben, dessen Vorsitzender er ist.

Michael Lahr
Program Director of Elysium and Executive Director of The Lahr von Leïtis Academy & Archive, studied philosophy in Munich and Paris. He curated the exhibit *Erwin Piscator: Political Theater in Exile,* which so far has been seen in Bernried, New York, Catania, Salzburg, and Munich. He has unearthed numerous works by artists who had to flee their home country under the pressure of the Nazi regime, or who were murdered.

Programmdirektor von Elysium und Executive Director von *The Lahr von Leïtis Academy & Archive,* studierte Philosophie in München und Paris. Er ist Kurator der Ausstellung *Erwin Piscator: Politisches Theater im Exil,* die bislang in Bernried, New York, Catania, Salzburg und München zu sehen war. Er hat zahlreiche Werke von Künstlern ausgegraben, die unter dem Druck des Nazi-Regimes ihre Heimat verlassen mussten oder ermordet wurden.

© des Buches 2013
Elysium – between two continents
The Lahr von Leïtis Academy & Archive
Bonner Platz 1
D-80803 München
www.elysiumbtc.org
www.lahrvonleitisacademy.eu

Editorial Assistance | Redaktionelle Mitarbeit:
Karin von Bülow

English Language Consultant:
Christine Schurtman

Layout & Graphic Design |
Layout & Graphische Gestaltung:
Alice Russo design

Printed by | Druck:
Fuchs Druck GmbH Miesbach

Printed in Germany
ISBN: 978-3-9816119-0-8

The printing of this book was supported by |
Mit freundlicher Unterstützung von:
Maren Otto
Falke KGaA – Paul Falke
Max Kade Foundation
Anna-Maria & Stephen Kellen Foundation
Jolana Blau
Anne-Marie Jacobs
Alexandra Kauka Hamill
Dr. Antje-Katrin Kühnemann
Dr. Bernd-A. von Maltzan
Eckbert von Bohlen und Halbach
Dr. Hans-Michael & Almut Giesen
Hans-Joachim und Monika Kippe
Rose Marie Gräfin von Königsdorff
Hans-Reinhardt Latten & Arnet Beyer
Prof. Dr. Jürgen & Eva-Barbara Ohlen
Jan-Peter P. & Tatjana Schacht
Paul B. Grosse & Maria-Anna Alp
Drs. Peter & Ellen Hedda Landesmann

Photo credits | Photonachweis

Photographer: Number of Page, (Number of Image) |
Photograph: Seitenzahl, (Nummer des Bildes)

Dario Acosta: 171
Dr. Steffen Amann: 109
Raffaelo Bencini: 4
Sarah Bicknell: 163, 166
Ralf Brinkhoff: 39
Victor Carnuccio: 45, 51, 60, 61, 67, 69, 73, 74
Carin Drechsler-Marx: 14, 94, 95, 102, 103, 108, 116, 117, 130, 131, 147, 173 174, 175, 184, 185
Gretchen Farrar: 142, 143
Felix Flemmer: 109 (No. 8)
Timothy Greenfield-Sanders: 145
Collection Louise Kerz Hirschfeld: 7
Paul Kolnik: 181
Michael Lahr: 153, 159 (No. 10), 175 (No. 12)
Lahr von Leïtis Archiv: 10, 12, 32, 36, 37, 40, 48, 80, 122, 148, 149, 158, 159,
Chris Lee: 91
Letizia Mariotti: 190
Jack Mitchell: 65
Peter W. Nikolaus: 88
Marc Raboy: 53
Silvia Ruhdorfer: 160
Joanne Savio: 125
Gisela Scheidler: 35
Steve J. Sherman: 151
Jerry Speier: 139
H. G. Simonis: 87
Dr. Konstanze Streese: 22, 29
Nic Tenwiggenhorn: 59
Bernd Uhlig: 31
Bryan Whitney: 55
Peter Wurst: 43

Cover Design by | Umschlaggestaltung:
Alice Russo design:
using Erwin Piscator's Silhouette and a stage design of Traugott Müller for the production of
Hoppla, wir leben! | unter Verwendung von Erwin Piscators Silhouette um 1927 und eines
Bühnenbildentwurfes von Traugott Müller für *Hoppla, wir leben!*